T0248353

(re)Made In America

An Immigrant's Journey to the American Dream

FABIAN BELLO

AYLESBURY
PUBLISHING

ISBN 978-0-9846887-6-0

eBook and Audiobook are available

For information about *special discounts* for bulk purchases, please contact *Aylesbury Publishing:*
www.AylesburyPublishing.com

First Edition
10 9 8 7 6 5 4 3 2 1

To my family.

Without you, I am nothing.

- Fabian Bello

CONTENTS

CHAPTER 1

Flight to Freedom

"The truth is there was no way in hell we were going back!"

Although I was born on September 2, 1976, my story really begins in 1946, the year my parents were born. My father, Gerardo Bello, and mother, Leyda Machado, were both born in Havana, Cuba, to upper-middle-class families. My father's family were poultry distributors, and my mother's family owned beauty salons. They were hardworking, prosperous people who had nice homes and lived comfortable lives. My mother and father recall happy, carefree childhoods where they didn't lack for anything. The Havana of my parents' childhood was a beautiful, vibrant city, and Cuba was one of the most advanced and successful Latin American countries. Cubans enjoyed a high literacy rate, educated a proportionally large number of doctors, and boasted a thriving middle class with the potential for upward mobility. Unfortunately, all of that changed when Fidel Castro assumed military and political power in 1959. All of my family's hopes and dreams for the future laid in the hands of a ruthless dictator, and the results were devastating.

Changes to daily life after the revolution were shocking. *"Patria o Muerte"* ("Country or Death") was the new slogan, and muerte it truly was for anyone who voiced opposition. The new government confiscated businesses, including my father's family poultry distribution business and my mother's family beauty salons; imprisoned dissenters; and began indoctrinating youth. A blanket of fear weighed heavily upon the Cuban people, and whispered conversations around the dinner table became a nightly ritual. *How long would the situation last? Could this government be overturned in the next election, or was this the new normal? Who had left Cuba? How bad could things get? Who would be the next to flee?* These questions and many others dominated conversations as ordinary Cuban citizens tried to make sense of the situation.

As part of claiming total power and authority, the government did all they could to remove the influence of God and religion as guiding beacons in the lives of the people. To fill the void, they promoted Castro's revolution and the doctrines of Communism as the highest moral authority. Although churches were still present in communities, participation in religious services was highly discouraged and in some cases, severely punished. Those who refused to give up religion were sent to a concentration camp called UMAP (Unidad Militar de Ayuda Produccion), where the guilty were sentenced to serve hard agricultural labor.

Havana was a large city, and a person was less likely to be persecuted for religious activities there unless someone specifically snitched on them or went out of their way to make life difficult for others. Life in the countryside, however, was not as easy. My dad's cousin, who lived in a small town, was observed by Communist zealots going in and out of church and was sent to UMAP for a three-year sentence. It was also not uncommon to receive a telegram instructing an individual to report for military service, but when you got there, you were really sent to the labor camp, which was the case with my dad's cousin. Unsurprisingly, religious persecution led society to reject common values. As families struggled to survive, ideals such as "thou shalt not steal" and other moral values became inconsequential. This deterioration led to the rise of alternative spiritual practices such as Santeria because its rituals could be performed easily in hiding. In the end, it was simply much easier for people to give in to the government's demands and abandon their faith altogether.

Life under the new Castro regime also limited self-determination for young adults, especially young men. When boys reached the age of fifteen, they were required to enter military service, which didn't officially end until they turned twenty-seven. During these years, they were deeply immersed and indoctrinated in the principles and practices of Communism. Additionally, when students graduated college with a degree, they were considered valuable assets of the state and were therefore prohibited from leaving Cuba. It was simply absurd to think that the Cuban Communist government would educate students and then allow them to leave and enrich another nation. The government's reach into the personal lives of its citizens grew in strength as personal liberty diminished.

My mother's family was the first in my extended family to leave Cuba. They left the country in stages, with my grandfather Osualdo being the first to flee in 1967. Osualdo had been politically active with counterrevolutionary groups and activities, and was arrested by the Castro regime, a frightening memory my mother can still recall today. Government officials searched their home looking for evidence to convict Osualdo, and when they found none, they were forced to let him go. If any incriminating evidence against him had been found, he would have been imprisoned, and his entire family would have been in terrible danger and permanently marked. In order to protect himself and his family, Osualdo went into hiding after his arrest. Fortunately, Osualdo had a sister living in Miami, Florida, who did all she could to get him out of Cuba. Leaving Cuba and his family behind was difficult, but staying was not an option. The danger to himself and his family was very real as several of his counterrevolutionary friends had been executed.

Because of his sister's efforts, Osualdo was able to immigrate directly to Miami from Cuba as a political refugee. At the time he immigrated, Miami was predominantly English speaking. Osualdo was there only a short while before he decided that he didn't like the language barrier, so he chose to move to Puerto Rico because it was Spanish speaking and closely resembled Cuban culture before the Castro revolution. He was able to open and operate a successful beauty salon there, but unfortunately, being separated from his wife took a toll on their relationship, and their marriage did not survive.

Three years after my grandfather Osualdo left, my grandmother Juanita was able to leave Cuba with her daughter Miriam and her youngest son, Alex. They immigrated directly to the United States and settled in Miami. My mother and her younger brother Osualdo did not go with them. At that point, my mother was engaged to marry my father, and Osualdo was of military age and therefore not permitted to leave the country. Their departure was yet another splinter as the slow family exodus continued.

The first time my father seriously considered escaping Cuba occurred in 1966, when he was twenty years old. In order to avoid active military service, he had enrolled in a maritime academy to learn the fundamentals of sailing, with the intention of possibly becoming a captain. One day, while on a training exercise in the Gulf of Mexico, my father's boat encountered severe weather and was forced to shelter in Cabo Contoy to avoid the worst of the storm. They weren't the only boat to seek shelter in that area. Many boats, including two vessels belonging to an American fishing company, were there. The vessels were all close to each other, and when my father realized that his boat was only twenty or thirty feet from the American fishing vessels, he seriously considered jumping into the water and swimming to them to seek asylum. He stood frozen on the deck, torn between his desire for freedom and his duty to family. Jumping into the ocean would have brought unwanted attention to his family and possibly ruin their chances to leave Cuba in the future. The moment passed and my father stayed on his boat, but he never forgot the names of the vessels that might have saved him: the *Coral Free* and the *Thunderbird*.

When my father returned home for the weekend after being so close to freedom, he burst into the living room, where his father was sitting. He pointed a finger at his father and said, "Yesterday I was less than twenty feet from freedom, but I didn't jump because I didn't want to jeopardize the possibility for anyone else in the family to leave. I suggest you start the paperwork to get out of here now because next time, I won't hesitate." Seeing the determination in my father's face, my grandfather agreed to move forward with the necessary paperwork to leave the country.

Two years later, on December 18, 1968, after obtaining the necessary paperwork, my grandfather and Uncle Rolando (my father's younger brother and only sibling) left Cuba and flew to Madrid, Spain. My uncle Rolando was permitted to leave because he was fourteen years old and not yet of military age. It was important for the family to get Rolando out of Cuba quickly because he was only three months shy of turning fifteen, which would automatically trigger his military training. The correct paperwork had been obtained for my grandmother as well, but she made the difficult decision to stay because my fa-

ther was twenty-two, which was military age, and therefore
he was not permitted to leave. His military obligation would
not end until he was twenty-seven, at which time he and his
mother planned to leave Cuba and reunite the family. It was a very
difficult choice to split the family. They parted knowing there
was a very real chance that they would never see each other again.

Rolando and my grandfather had to travel to Spain
because at that time, emigrating directly from Cuba to the
United States was not possible. Cuban immigrants needed to
travel to another country, request refugee status, and then apply
to enter the United States from that second country. Spain was a
good choice because at that time, Spain was issuing visas to the
United States after applicants were in the country for only one
week on the proviso that they would not settle permanently in
Spain. My uncle and grandfather's planned one-week stay for the
travel visa turned into a five-year wait because so many people
were attempting to enter the United States through Spain. To
support themselves while they waited, my grandfather worked as
a mover, and Uncle Rolando delivered wine and spirits throughout the city and even washed dishes at night. Rolando was not
able to attend school because he needed to work, but later on, he
was able to take a computing class, which would ultimately lead
to a career in computer programming. A year later, my grandfather got a better job with benefits working in shipping for a
pharmaceutical company. They spent almost four and a half years
in Spain before my uncle Rolando finally got a visa to go to the
United States in April of 1973. My grandfather joined him in

Miami a few months later. When they left Cuba, my grandfather and uncle could never have anticipated that the move to Spain, which would ultimately lead them to the United States, would separate the family for eleven long years.

My father's second attempt to escape Cuba occurred in the early months of 1969, about two months after my grandfather and Uncle Rolando had left for Spain. My father and mother were both studying English at a home in my mother's neighborhood, which is where they met, and had been dating for a few months. Desperate to escape, my father and his trusted friend Juan built a very small boat consisting of six twenty-five-gallon containers (three on each side) topped by wood planks held together with metal straps. They removed the bed frame and placed the mattress directly on top of the small boat, concealing it from their parents and any other prying eyes. One night, dressed in black, they pulled the boat out from under the bed and, with the help of my mother and Juan's girlfriend, transported the boat to the beach, where they planned to depart. The girls were a critical part of the escape plan because if they were stopped and questioned for any reason, they could pretend they were on a date. Once everything was set, they said good-bye and the girls left. Their families had no idea what they were doing. Secrecy was vital because they were leaving the island illegally, and they didn't want any of their remaining family to have any prior knowledge of their plans. It was their way of protecting the people they loved in case they were caught.

My father and Juan launched the boat in the dead of

night, but they were only able to travel about a mile off the coast before the waves became too rough and the small boat capsized. In reality, the boat was not equipped to sail on the open ocean. To begin with, the boat was tiny and inadequate for the task. It was smaller than the bed it was hidden under, much too small to handle rough seas. In the end, the boat took on large amounts of water, causing it to list wildly and knocking all of their drinking water and food supplies overboard. As the boat was sinking, Juan was overcome with fear. He panicked and refused to abandon the craft to swim to shore. He simply froze. My father had to get in his face and snap him out of it. It was a desperate situation, but thankfully Juan recovered enough to make it back to shore with my father's continuous and forceful encouragement every step of the way. If they had bothered to assess the situation logically, they would have known that they didn't stand a chance. In reality, the entire episode was doomed to fail, but it demonstrated just how desperate my father and Juan were to be free. Their failure was a terrible disappointment to them at the time, and they never spoke about it after that evening. As for me, I see their failure that night as divine intervention in my father's life. It was as if God were saying, "No, not this way. This is *not* your time." If it hadn't been for those waves, I wouldn't be here today, and you would be reading a different story.

After the failed escape, my parents began dating seriously and decided to marry when they were both twenty-three. My parents wanted a church wedding, which was severely frowned upon by the government. In fact, when my father's boss at Ferrocarriles de Cuba (Cuba Railroads) learned they were planning a church wedding, he called him into the office and reminded him that getting married in church—or even going to church—ran contrary to Communism and its ideals. If they continued with their plans, they ran the risk of being sent to UMAP (the concentration camp where people who refused to denounce religion were sent). Nevertheless, they were determined and stuck with their desire to do things their way. My parents had a strong belief in God, and my mother was a staunch Catholic. They wanted to be married by a priest in a church and in the presence of God. This was particularly important to my mother as she believed in the traditional strictures of a Christian courtship and had committed to remaining virtuous before marriage. Of course, it would have been much easier for my parents to choose to be married civilly, but they were determined not to let Communism erase their religious beliefs or the traditions and sacraments of their faith. In the end, nobody turned them in, and on December 6, 1969, they were married in Iglesia de la Merced, the most popular Catholic church in Havana. It was not the wedding they had hoped for from an attendance perspective because many friends and family had already left Cuba, including my mother's father who didn't get to walk his daughter down the isle. And yet, despite all of the discouragement they received, it was the Catholic wedding they chose for themselves.

Once married, my parents moved into my mother's family home. The home was large and registered under Osualdo's name (my mother's younger brother), but he was in military service at the time and not home consistently. Although the family in Cuba was small, they were all very supportive of each other and helped one another in any way they could. My grandmother Obdulia (my father's mother) worked as a secretary and continued living in the Bello home. My mother stayed home, anchoring the family, while my father continued working at Cuban Railroads as a statistician. My father was paid 81.50 pesos every two weeks, which was the equivalent of about eighty dollars. It was not a lot of money. To put his salary in perspective, a box of cigarettes cost 50 pesos (more than half of my father's two-week salary) on the black market at that time. Even though everyone received food rations from the government, it was never enough, and anything not included in the rations had to be purchased on the black market or sourced through personal connections.

My parents wanted children, but they were reluctant to start a family while living under a Communist regime. They did all they could to legally migrate to the United States prior to committing to having children. They always expected that when my father turned twenty-seven and his period of military commitment was complete, he would be allowed to leave, but when that time came, the Castro government had modified their policy, making it extremely difficult for anyone to leave regardless of age, especially between the years 1970 and 1978. This was a major setback for my parents and grandmother, but by this point, my grandfather and Uncle Rolando were in the

United States and were working diligently with my mother's family in Florida to bring the rest of the family over. Unfortunately, things move very slowly in Communist systems, and the process ended up taking several years. My parents had been married for seven years when my mother finally decided they couldn't wait any longer to have children. She was thirty years old and felt that time was running out, so they agreed to start their family even if it meant that a baby would be born in Communist Cuba.

* * * * *

I was born in Havana on September 2, 1976. Having a child was bittersweet for my parents. On the one hand, they were extremely grateful to have a healthy baby, but on the other, they were worried about what the future held for us if they were not able to leave Cuba. From the day I was born, my parents did everything they could to shield me from the realities of Communism. In order to ensure that I had enough milk and protein to be healthy and develop properly, my parents and my grandmother Obdulia, whom we lovingly call Yuya, dedicated all of their food rations for my use. My parents and grandmother then obtained simpler food such as plantains, rice, potatoes, and bread on the black market for themselves. Fortunately, my father had a friend who lived in the country and owned a cow, and he brought my father fresh milk every day for me to drink. Having fresh milk daily meant that the tinned or powdered milk from the ration cards could be stored for future use, and meat rations were frozen and used to make baby food. This sounds extreme, but only households with children were entitled to milk rations, which for one child was not enough to make a bottle of milk per day, a potentially devastating situation for families with small children. My family's love and determination sustained me through my infant years in Cuba, and I am grateful for their devotion. Because of their resourcefulness and willingness to sacrifice for me, I never suffered from hunger or malnutrition as so many other children did at that time.

My birth intensified my parents' determination to flee Cuba. My father's weekly visits to the government agency that processed and approved all immigration requests increased to near-daily visits, but in the end, getting out was a group effort. Having family established in the United States drastically increased our chances of leaving. My grandfather and Uncle Rolando paid the fees required by the Cuban government, and they assumed financial responsibility for us so they could prove to the United States government that we would not be dependent on government services when we arrived. In the end, everyone's efforts paid off, and six months after my second birthday, we were granted the visas we needed to finally leave Cuba. We would follow the same path my grandfather and Uncle Rolando had forged and travel to Spain. Once in Spain, we would apply for the proper paperwork to legally enter the United States and finally reunite with my grandfather, my uncle

Rolando, my grandmother Juanita, my aunt Miriam, and my uncle Alex in Miami.

Even though my parents were overjoyed at the opportunity to immigrate to the United States, the realities of leaving Cuba were sobering. Prior to leaving, my family was required to forfeit all of their belongings, including all valuable and cherished possessions. Officials carefully inventoried each item and required signed documents stating that ownership of the items was being voluntarily transferred to the government. On our day of departure, we were allowed to pack only one suitcase of clothing each, a rule we adhered to strictly because anyone caught trying to smuggle any items of value out of Cuba risked having their visa revoked on the spot. The most difficult part of leaving, however, was parting with loved ones. Imagine the pain my great-grandparents felt as all of their children, grandchildren, and great-grandchildren fled Cuba. Now imagine that pain repeated over and over again throughout the years. The only balm to their pain was knowing that their children, grandchildren, and great-grandchildren would live in freedom in the United States.

My father, mother, Yuya, and I left Cuba on May 20, 1979. We boarded a Super DC-8 plane in Havana operated by Iberia Airlines. The flight originated in Costa Rica, with a brief layover in Cuba, where we were scheduled to board and would then continue on to Madrid, Spain. Tensions were high as the boarding process began. Government officials monitored every step of the departure process and at any moment could deny anyone the right to leave. In fact, it was not uncommon for people to be pulled out of line while ascending the stairs to the plane and have their permission to travel revoked. My parents and Yuya had forfeited all of their items to the government two days prior, so if anything had gone wrong and we were denied the right to travel for any reason, they would have lost everything. It was critical to not do anything that would draw any unwanted attention from the Cuban officials overseeing the boarding process. Nobody was truly safe until they were on the plane and in the air. The final paperwork was turned over at the bottom of the stairs leading up to the plane. My father carried me up the stairs, and before entering, he turned and held me high above his head, facing Cuba, and defiantly whispered, "You will not have my son!"

I have very faint memories of that day. I know my mother and father were sitting together towards the aircraft's midsection, while Yuya and I were seated at the back. I also remember having a little Pluto plush toy that Yuya twirled by the ears throughout the flight to keep me entertained. The moments before takeoff were particularly tense for my mother. The fear and anxiety of being denied travel weighed very heavily on her, and shortly after takeoff, she became overwhelmed and fainted. Crew members laid her on the floor by the emergency exit, and as they worked to revive her, the captain was called out to assess the situation. His initial thought was that the plane should return to Cuba so my mother could receive medical attention. My father realized that if our family returned to Cuba, we might never have the opportunity to leave again, so he assured the captain that my mother was in excellent health and would be fine. He explained the stress of leaving and how overwhelming the day had been. The captain understood and had compassion. He agreed to trust my father's judgment, and the flight continued. The truth is there was no way in hell we were going back! Eight hours later, our family arrived in Spain, and four months after that, on September 27, 1979—twenty-five days after my third birthday—we arrived in the United States. Our flight to freedom was finally complete.

CHAPTER 2

Becoming American

"In the United States, there is always a pathway to achieving the American Dream."

We arrived in Miami on September 27, 1979, just three days after my third birthday. Words can never fully describe the happiness my parents felt when finally reuniting with family who were already living in the United States. Even though I was very young, I remember the joy and intense love felt within our family. My grandfather Gerardo and my uncle Rolando were finally reunited with Yuya and my father after an eleven-year separation. My mother was reunited with her mother (my grandmother Juanita); her sister, Miriam; and her youngest brother, Alex. Our family had also grown. Uncle Rolando had married Rosa, a Cuban immigrant, and their first child, Rolando Jr., was only a few weeks old when we arrived. In our absence, my maternal and paternal families had met, and a close bond had developed as they worked together to get us out of Cuba and make sure we had the money we needed to live during our four-month stay in Madrid, Spain. The only person missing from our reunited family aside from my great-grandparents was my uncle Osualdo, my mother's brother, who had stayed in Cuba because he was still of military age. He would eventually join the family in the United States in 1992.

My maternal grandmother, Juanita, had been living in a small two-bedroom apartment, but when we arrived, she made arrangements to move to a different apartment so we would have a place to live. She had also generously paid for the first few months' rent to help us get on our feet financially. The apartment was a furnished two-bedroom, one-bath unit and was very comfortable for our small family. Our house in Cuba had been much larger, but what good is a big house unless you have the freedom to truly enjoy it? It was our first home in the United States, and I still distinctly remember the cool air and the gentle humming from the in-wall air conditioner in the bedroom. It was a reassuring, comforting sound that I still find calming when I travel today.

A few days after our arrival, my father got his first job. He was hired to repaint the Spanish tile roof of a one-story apartment building. I remember walking to the apartment complex with my mother to watch him work. I felt a strong sense of pride and admiration watching him work hard for our family. To me he was a giant on that roof, and in my eyes, no one could ever be as tall or as important as my father. He taught me through his example to work hard, take pride in honest work, and ensure that the job is well done. It is a lesson that still guides me in all I do.

Shortly after completing the roof job, my father was offered a full-time job at People's Gas, now known as Teco Energy, as an LP gas delivery driver. But as one door opened, another closed. The landlord of our apartment complex was a New Yorker who didn't like kids, and unbeknownst to my family, the lease agreement clearly stated that no children were allowed to live in the apartment. When he found out that I was living in the apartment, he kicked us out. Luckily, we were quickly able to find housing in a different apartment complex. I called our new place the "rat complex" because one day I found a mortally injured rat outside our front door. I felt sorry for the rat and stopped to caress it as its eyelids slowly closed and died. When my mother noticed what I was doing, she screamed, rushed me inside, and vigorously scrubbed my hands with soap and alcohol. Unsurprisingly, that memory is the only clear one I have from living in that apartment complex.

After our move to the new apartment in early 1980, my mother started working with her sister, Miriam, at the headquarters and main distribution center for Luria's, a large home goods retail chain store in South Florida. It was a good job in an exclusive area, and my mother enjoyed the work. She had an excellent work ethic and quickly became a trusted employee, so much so that she was assigned to price, tag, and sort the jewelry that would later be distributed to all their stores. While both of my parents worked, I was looked after in day care.

While life in the United States was stable and safe, living conditions in Cuba were worsening. Cuba under the Castro regime was experiencing job and housing shortages caused by a struggling economy and political unrest. On April 20, 1980, Castro announced that any Cuban who wanted to leave the island would be allowed to go, and he opened the borders. Cuban Americans rushed to hire boats to rescue family members in Cuba. The boats set sail from South Florida and docked at the Port of Mariel in Havana, which is where all Cubans who wanted to leave boarded the boats. The Mariel boatlift, as the exodus was called, lasted six months and resulted in the mass migration of 125,000 Cubans to the United States and other surrounding countries.

The Cuban American community in Florida welcomed the *Marielitos*, as the refugees came to be known, but the large influx of people into South Florida impacted the economy. In May of 1980, as a direct result of the Mariel boatlift, our rent went up one hundred dollars, a nearly 25 percent rise. In early spring, my mother also discovered that she was pregnant again. It was surprising but exciting news for my parents because doctors had told my mother that it was unlikely she would be able to have another child. The rent increase, along with our soon becoming a family of four, presented a challenge to my parents, who were still adjusting to their new life in the United States and trying to establish themselves financially. A new path needed to be blazed if our family were to survive in America.

My parents were at a crossroads. They could continue on the path they were on and both continue working, but my father calculated that my mother's income would cover only the cost of clothes, childcare, and transportation to and from work, with little to nothing left over. With another baby on the way, childcare costs would double, but my mother's salary would not. On that economic path, my parents would not only struggle to get by, but they would also never build wealth, a situation so many people find themselves in today. In order to change their future, our family needed to make sacrifices. My father carefully thought about our evolving situation and came up with a bold plan. He secured an $8,000 loan from his father to buy a mobile home in Homestead, Florida. Both my parents agreed that the most important job my mother could have was being home to raise their children, so my mother quit her job and committed to being a full-time homemaker. In exchange, my father planned to work multiple jobs to increase their household income to get ahead. So, in addition to working full time at People's Gas Systems, when he got off of work at 4:30 p.m., he worked for International Equipment refurbishing restaurant appliances until 8:30 p.m. On weekends, he would occasionally work overtime at People's Gas. My father worked at People's Gas until he retired in 2009 and kept the second job at International Equipment through 1987. During that seven-year time frame, he worked more than sixty-five hours a week.

Changing our family's financial situation was a team effort for my parents. My mother could never have stayed home to raise children and manage the family's physical and emotional needs without my father's excellent work ethic and willingness to work. My father could not have found the strength and determination to work so hard without my mother's unwavering support and confidence. They were a winning team and always worked in harmony to raise me and my brother while also putting the time and effort in to meet each other's needs. They understood that nothing comes without sacrifice, and if getting ahead meant living in a trailer park for a while, they were willing to do it.

My brother, Sanders, was born on September 8, 1980, six days after I turned four. When I first learned a baby was on the way, I wasn't very excited to have a sibling, but that changed after Sanders was born. My parents did a good job preparing me to be a good big brother, and I took my role seriously. Sanders and I shared a room, and if he cried in the night or during naps, I would jump up and pat him on his butt to soothe him back to sleep. Like most American children in the 1980s, I had a great interest in all things Disney. I loved the characters in books, TV shows, and movies. I also had a lot of Disney records and a small record player. I liked to entertain Sanders by playing records for him, often showing him the books that went along with the records. I genuinely loved being a big brother and always did my best to emulate the love and devotion my parents modeled for us. My love for my brother has persisted throughout my life. It is a role I will always cherish.

My father's plan was put into action when we moved to Homestead in January of 1981. Our new home was a single-wide trailer with two bedrooms and one bathroom. It was fifty-two feet long and fifteen feet wide, but it didn't feel small to us. In fact, there was a large screened-in porch that was about twenty-five feet long and fifteen feet wide that ran along the side of the trailer, which made it feel larger than the apartment we had been renting. The kitchen was at the front of the trailer, and it had a large freezer that was always stocked with food. We might have lacked some resources, but we were never without food. My parents had a lot of pride in their new home. My father repaired the trailer and gave it a fresh coat of paint, removed the carpet, and installed linoleum floors. My mother kept the trailer what I affectionally call "Cuban clean," an exaggerated, over-the-top standard of cleanliness. Our little home was meticulously kept, comfortable, and full of love. Living in a trailer might have felt like a major downgrade for a lot of people, but not for us. My parents had a plan, and they were committed to making the best of the situation while maintaining a strong feeling of gratitude for the opportunity to change their circumstances.

My mother took the move to the trailer in stride. The move affected her the most because not only had she given up her job and had a new baby, but she suddenly found herself alone at home all day and late into the evenings with two small children. Instead of feeling sorry for herself or becoming resentful, my mother embraced the changes and found meaning in her new role as a full-time mother of two. Looking back, I'm not surprised; my mother has always been the type of person who adjusts quickly to the realities of whatever circumstance she's in. Of course there were struggles. One challenge was that our trailer park was located in a small community and surrounded by farmland. Even though she was willing to be there, she didn't always feel safe living in a what my parents lovingly referred to as a "tin can." Someone tried to break in once, and after that scare, my father purchased a gun and had my mother take shooting lessons. No one ever tried to break in again, but if they had, I have no doubt that my mother would not have hesitated to defend our family.

I didn't speak any English at the time of our move, but that didn't stop me from making friends. I specifically remember Brent and Charles, two brothers who lived in our trailer park. They were my first friends in the United States, and their friendship meant a lot to me. I often wonder where they are today and have tried searching for them, but I don't recall their last name, which has made finding them extremely difficult. We spent a lot of time together climbing trees, playing in the park, and roaming the tomato fields around our trailer park. It was a welcome change to being in childcare, and I enjoyed the freedom of being outdoors. My mother didn't do as well making friends in our little community. Both of my parents were committed to integrating into American culture, but speaking English proved to be very difficult for them. They could both read English rather well, and they never expected anyone to make exceptions for them, but the language barrier proved to be embarrassing to them, which made friendships with native English speakers challenging. In the absence of friends, our extended family filled the social void. On weekends, we would always either go to see family, or they would come to us. My parents committed themselves to living very frugally to meet their financial goals, so we never did anything that cost money other than going to the grocery store. They would cook inexpensive traditional Cuban food and then sit around sharing stories and memories as well as strategizing and discussing what they needed to do to succeed in the United States. It was a strong, loving support system rooted firmly in reality.

I don't remember learning English. As with so many other immigrant children, learning a second language came quickly and naturally to me from being immersed in school and playing with friends, and by the end of first grade in 1983, I was fluent. It was also at the end of first grade that my parents had saved enough money to buy a new family home in the middle-class community of Hialeah, Florida. They sold the mobile home for $14,000 and had been able to save an additional $20,000, which allowed them to place a significant down payment on a newly constructed, three-bedroom, two-bath 2,000-square-foot home that they bought for $76,000. Our new home was a palace compared to our mobile home. I can still remember the day we moved in. My mother cried tears of joy, and my father was so proud of what he had been able to achieve after being in the United States only four years. Sanders and I had our own rooms, which made us feel like royalty. I was young, but I understood the importance of this major change for our family. I was so proud of my dad and grateful to have a devoted mother who was completely dedicated to our happiness. Together, they taught me that a goal can be reached through careful planning, hard work and determination, and a willingness to sacrifice coupled with humbly acknowledging the blessings that we already had.

My parents loved their new life in the United States, and they could see the pathway to achieving the American Dream. They loved being free, free to do what they wanted with their lives, free to go where they wanted, and free to work where they wanted to work. Of course, there were occasional challenges and disappointments along the way, but whenever a problem arose, my parents would ask themselves, "Is this something we would rather be back in Cuba over?" The answer to that question was always a resounding "No!" Whatever the challenge was, they always found a solution and embraced a positive outlook and approach.

From the moment we arrived in Florida, our family was completely committed to being American. Becoming American citizens had been the dream that had sustained my parents through all of the difficult years in Cuba, and five years after we arrived, as soon as my parents qualified, they applied for and in due time were granted United States citizenship. Their swearing-in occurred on July 4, 1986, at the Miami Orange Bowl. The swearing-in ceremony and message was done via satellite from the Statue of Liberty. Ronald Reagan, who was president at the time, participated in the broadcast, which made it even more exciting. My brother and I were there, dressed in our Sunday best. Sanders had been born in the United States and was therefore already a citizen, but because I had been born in Cuba and still a minor,

I became a citizen when my parents did. Even though I was ten years old at the time, I fully understood the importance of that day for me too. I remember feeling a deep sense of pride and gratitude as I watched my parents. They had sacrificed literally everything they had to get to the United States and then took advantage of every opportunity this country afforded them to be successful in their own way. In both situations, their risk and hard work had paid off. They happily denounced their allegiance to Cuba and wholeheartedly embraced American citizenship. They had worked so hard and sacrificed so much for us all to become Americans.

CHAPTER 3

Strength through Adversity

*"I might have been only seven, but in that moment,
I knew that the world could be cruel and unfair."*

I distinctly remember my first day of school in the United States. The year was 1981, but even after all this time, if I close my eyes and think about it, I still feel nervous. I had never attended preschool or any other pre-K programs other than the few months of day care when we first arrived in the United States. All I had known up to that point of my life was my mother's constant love and protection and my father's steady influence. My world was as big as our small trailer.

My parents enrolled me in Naranja Elementary in Homestead, Florida, which was close to our trailer park, but I still had to take the bus to get there. Every morning, my mother walked me the short distance to the closest bus stop. The giant yellow school bus was terrifying to me, and I remember fighting my mother about getting on by myself for the first time. Despite all of my desperate protestations, she wrestled me on, firmly placed me on a seat, and insisted I cut it out. There was no way I was not going to school. I stopped fighting after that because I knew how important school was to my mother, and nothing was ever going to change her mind about it. I didn't like the bus because I didn't know any of the other kids, and the driver was always changing. When we arrived at the school on the first day, I felt lost and abandoned. I had no idea where I was or how to get to class, which was overwhelming and incredibly scary, especially for a child who didn't speak English well.

The first few days of school at Naranja were difficult. The principal was a white American man who was very intimidating, especially to small children. I especially remember him walking around campus smacking a wooden paddle against his hand. I was raised in a strict home, so that paddle made a big impression on me and kept me on my best behavior. I had no interest in being on the receiving end of that paddle. Luckily, both my kindergarten and first grade teachers were Cuban women. They were kind and dedicated to their job. They dealt with students in a loving, maternal way, which helped me feel at ease. When I started school, I didn't speak much English, but as is common for a lot of young children, I learned quickly. Playing with my friends at school and in the trailer park also really helped with language development. My parents were pleased with my progress and proud to see me becoming a little American. Most of all, they were happy I had the opportunity to go to school in a free country and have the opportunity to determine my own future.

We moved to our new house in Hialeah the summer after I finished first grade. We spent the summer adjusting to our new home and neighborhood, but as the summer ended, I became sick with anxiety, nausea, and diarrhea at the thought of starting over at a new school. I didn't have to ride the public school bus, which I was happy about, but instead, my parents arranged for me to take a private bus to school with about a dozen other kids, driven by a Cuban woman named Yoya. However, another problem soon emerged. The bus wasn't air-conditioned, and the constant stop-and-go movement made me ill. I spent most mornings and afternoons sitting in the front seat begging Yoya to pull over so I could open the door and throw up.

The first day of second grade did not go well. My teacher, Mrs. Harris, wasn't Cuban, and I immediately sensed that she didn't like her job. She yelled a lot, which was scary, and often punished students in ways that would be illegal today. I remember thinking that she didn't like me because I was Cuban, which may or may not have been true, but I was certain she didn't like children.

The first thing we did was go around the room and introduce ourselves. We had to stand up and state our name and age, and if we were new to the school, state what school we had attended the previous year. I was very nervous about this exercise. As everyone took their turn, I practiced in my mind how to introduce myself in English. When it was my turn, I immediately sensed by the tone of her voice and her overall demeanor that Mrs. Harris was annoyed. I was very nervous and trembling, but I stood up and said, "My name is Fabian Bello. I am seven years old, and I came from Orange Elementary."

Mrs. Harris immediately jumped up and yelled, "Boy! No need for that nonsense in my class!" Everyone burst out laughing while I stood there shocked and embarrassed. I couldn't understand what I had done wrong. "There's no such thing as Orange Elementary, you clown!" she yelled and kicked me out of class.

I sat in the hall crying, trying to figure out where I had gone wrong. I had carefully chosen every word of my little speech and had practiced it at least a dozen times in my head before it was my turn. I had listened carefully to my classmates and tried hard to emulate their style of language. The problem was that as I was learning English, I would think of what I wanted to say in Spanish and then translate it, word for word, into English. My former school was Naranja Elementary, which translated to English is "Orange" Elementary. It never occurred to me that my elementary school had a Spanish name, as I translated all the Spanish words in my head, I had simply also translated naranja to orange without thinking about it. It was an innocent mistake and certainly not worthy of the extreme reaction I received.

A little while later, when the class went to art or music class, another boy (whose crime I don't recall) and I were brought back into the classroom and required to hold two heavy books flat on our hands, palms up, with our arms held out straight at our sides. We were forced to endure this punishment for about twenty minutes, although it felt like an eternity to me. In the moments when I thought I would collapse and wanted to break down crying, I remember thinking, If Jesus was in a similar position for hours nailed to a cross, then I should be able to make it through this just fine. I might have been only seven, but in that moment, I knew that the world could be cruel and unfair. I understood that it was up to me to endure my trials and find a way through them.

That event happened more than thirty-seven years ago, but I still think about Mrs. Harris's ignorance and cruelty. I know firsthand how difficult it is to navigate the world in two languages. It requires a high level of intelligence and sensitivity, and I would never dream of mocking a person, let alone a child, in that situation. I often wonder what happened to Mrs. Harris. I hope she was able to evolve and become a better person and teacher. She almost broke me that day, and although her behavior can never be justified, in retrospect, that experience made me stronger. Now, whenever I drive by an orange grove, I remember a scared little boy who refused to be broken.

Third and fourth grade passed in a blur, but one thing was clear: the older I got, the less loved and accepted I felt at school. Mrs. Delgado's fifth grade class was the exception, it was a welcomed reprieve in a sea of unhappiness. I was relieved to have a Cuban teacher (again) who was strict and had high expectations while at the same time being kind, fair, and genuinely interested in her students. She had a no bullying policy that she strictly enforced, and for the first time since leaving Naranja Elementary, I felt I actually had a chance to have a good year before moving on to what I expected to be a difficult middle school experience.

* * * * *

I started sixth grade at Jose Marti Middle School in the city of Hialeah Gardens, Florida in 1987. As anticipated, middle school was a nightmare. My parents did all they could to prepare me and impress upon me the importance of working hard and getting good grades. My father felt that middle school would be filled with serious students, but as anyone who has attended middle school in the public education system can tell you, his perception was far from the truth. In reality, very few students at Jose Marti took academics seriously. Good behavior was reserved for church, and my peers, in contrast, were mean and hateful, especially towards nerds. And I was a nerd. I was unathletic and average looking, and I had a hard time connecting with other boys my age. It was easier for me to interact with girls, and I had become friends with a few I could hang out with, but even then, middle school was a very lonely period of my life.

My father was adamant that I take classes that he personally felt were important for my future. One class he was particularly excited about was computer science. I didn't share his enthusiasm, so on the first day of school, I went to my counselor and changed computer science to band. When I came home from school and told my mother what I had done, we both knew that my father would be upset, but my mother understood my position and helped soften the blow with my father. My mother, like so many other good wives, brought out the softer side of my father and helped him see situations from other points of view, and my father was wise enough to listen to her and trust her judgment. She also helped me understand my father and explained his position in a way I could understand. Because of her, I was able to recognize how hard my father worked for our family and felt firsthand the love he had for me and my brother. No matter how hard life might have seemed, I never doubted my parents' love and devotion for me.

It turned out that the impromptu schedule change altered the course of my life and was the vehicle that made middle school bearable. Band was the only class I didn't hate, and it was the only motivation I had to get through the day. Band was a safe place for me. When everyone was banging on drums and I was learning to blow on a trumpet, I was able to push aside the insults, bullying, and endless name-calling I had endured daily since the third grade. I was only eight years old and in third grade when I was labeled a "fag." I knew that "fag" didn't necessarily refer to my sexuality. I was a young boy and totally innocent and unaware of such things. Instead, I understood that it was a word intended to belittle and describe an insignificant, worthless, and useless excuse for a boy. I was an impressionable young boy, so I believed it. After all, everyone else thought it was true, so why shouldn't I? The names and taunts were hard on their own, but

I was also frustrated and hurt because I desperately wanted to fit in with the other boys. I wanted to be a jock. I wanted to be cool and admired, but the reality was that I really wasn't interested in the things the other boys were interested in. I was a kind, sensitive, and loving little boy and totally unprepared to handle the bullying I experienced. The only meaningful friendships I had were with other girls my age. It wasn't necessarily ideal for me, but having predominantly female friends helped me learn how to listen and to understand girls. In time, I became the male friend the girls turned to for advice.

Throughout middle school, I always felt that if I couldn't find a way to deal with the bullying, then my only option would be to take my own life and end my misery. I was a sad, desperate boy who had a hard time believing that my situation would eventually change. I'm sure that my friends and family would be shocked if they knew how desperate I felt at that time and how badly the bullying affected me, especially my parents, who had no idea about what I was going through. Being young and inexperienced, I felt that I was the problem, and the only way to end the bullying was to end myself. I don't share this with the intent to be pitied but rather with the hope that my own experience may help someone else who has felt rejected and abused by their peers to know that they are not alone. There is *always* hope. I'm sure some may wonder why I didn't tell my parents about my suicidal thoughts. My response at that time would have been "Why should I do that?" It would have been humiliating to tell my dad that the entire school thought I was a "fag," and I thought that if I told him about the bullying, he would have been ashamed of and embarrassed by me. He worked so hard and sacrificed so much so we could have a chance to excel, and I thought that if he really knew what my peers thought of me, I would be a disgrace to his legacy. Looking back, I wish I had trusted and confided in my father. He certainly would have helped me through that difficult time in my life, but I didn't know him well enough at that age. To me, he was a trailblazer, a hero, and the epitome of a man's man—all the things I thought I could never be.

Luckily, and by the grace of God, I made it through my darkest hours, and things started to change at the end of seventh grade when I auditioned to be a band officer. I became cocaptain in eighth grade and band captain in ninth grade, my final year of middle school. My new role as band captain meant that I would conduct the band during warm-ups, performances and competitions. Having an identity was a huge boost to my confidence and allowed me to start shedding some of my doubts and insecurities. I was accepted and respected amongst the other band students, and it turned out I was good at my new role. My band director admired and acknowledged my leadership skills, which meant a lot to me, but even better, my bandmates started to treat me with kindness and respect. It was a new and wonderful feeling.

My four years of middle school eventually came to an end, and I had taken my share of bullying. I had been beaten up a couple of times, and my nose had been broken by a particularly disturbed boy. I had experienced loneliness and extreme lows, but I had made it through and had established a handful of incredible female friends, who are still part of my life today. There was finally a flicker of light at the end of the tunnel.

* * * * *

I started my sophomore year (tenth grade) at Hialeah Senior High School in the fall of 1991. I knew high school would be difficult, but I was optimistic that I was more prepared for high school than I had been for middle school. Of course, I joined the high school band and spent most of my time and energy practicing and preparing to be Drum Major. Being Drum Major was a goal I had been working towards after I saw my first marching band show during my last year in middle school. Leading the band out to perform and conducting the entire show was something I thought I would enjoy more than just playing my trumpet. It was an ambitious goal considering there had not been a male Drum Major at my high school for quite some time. I had to prove to myself, my bandmates, and the band director that I was capable and worthy of the role. My hard work paid off, and during my junior and senior years, I became the first male drum major at my school in over two decades. It was a role that changed my life. I wasn't athletic, I didn't excel academically, and I wasn't the most talented musician, but I learned that I was a good leader. It was a gift previously unknown to me, but once I realized my own leadership potential, I started thinking about myself differently. I felt useful and believed I could provide value to an organization and society.

Knowing others believe in you is very important. Just as I started realizing my own potential, I received a boost of confidence in an unexpected way. My best friend Marisa's mom often drove us to different functions, and one day while we were sitting in the car waiting for Marisa, we began talking about business and life. She told me, "I expect you'll have a penthouse in New York City one day. You'll make it big. I just know it." I was stunned. I had never considered such a thing, but hearing her say that was a massive boost to my confidence and a motivation to nurture my newfound abilities.

Another benefit of being in high school was that I grew a foot and started to tower over everyone. The bullying stopped, and I actually started to enjoy being at school. Of course, I experienced challenging and uncomfortable moments, but after all I had been through in middle school, it didn't seem like such a big deal. My physical and emotional growth made it possible for me to connect better with guys, and I was able to make some very good male friends. Most of all, I developed a strong sense that life was going to fall in place for me.

As my senior year came to a close, I was left thinking, *What the heck do I do now?* I was a C student with poor SAT scores and had minimal interest in academics. I knew I wasn't prepared or interested enough to be a doctor, lawyer, accountant, or engineer. I felt that business was a good option for me, but I wasn't a talented enough student to go to a Harvard, Oxford, or

NYU. I knew I had it in me to be great, but I wasn't sure what path would lead me there. My family has always been big on "keeping it real," and when I applied that principle to my own life, it was obvious that I wasn't ready to go to a university, so I enrolled at Miami Dade Community College and focused on learning to be a good student. Simultaneously, I had the opportunity to play trumpet for the University of Miami marching band. They allowed musicians from surrounding colleges to join their band to increase their numbers. It was a great opportunity for me and allowed me to experience the university environment while I was attending community college.

I started at Miami Dade with a large group of students who, for the most part, were struggling to get by, and over the course of two years, I watched the majority of them drop out. I had dropped a few classes over several semesters, and when I realized that I was starting to fall behind on credits, I asked myself, *What the hell am I doing here?* I got in my car, drove to the University of Miami, and met with an admissions counselor. I asked her what I needed to do to *get in* and then got back in my car, drove back to Miami Dade, and asked an academic counselor there what classes I needed to complete my associate's degree and *get out!* The next semester, I received special permission to take twenty-one credits at Miami Dade and then transferred to the University of Miami. When I got there, I was a semester behind compared to the students who had started school at the same time as I had, but I was committed to surrounding myself with serious students and staying on track to graduate within two years. I firmly believe that we are a product of our environment, and I was determined to never again allow myself to perform below my highest potential. I committed to surrounding myself with people who had similar values and who were striving for greatness. The University of Miami is a relatively small, elite private school, and I was distinctly aware of how fortunate I was to be there.

CHAPTER 4

A Time of Change

"Change must always be embraced as fuel to propel us forward."

I transferred to the University of Miami in January 1997. Although I had spent a significant amount of time on campus as a band member while attending community college, being an official UM student was a dream come true. From the very beginning, I knew I was different from most of the other students at the University of Miami. I hadn't been admitted because I was an exceptionally talented student, because I wasn't. My grades in high school and community college were average. However, I had just earned an Associate of Arts degree, which gave me priority admission as a transfer student, and I had also earned a very strong recommendation from the University of Miami band director, Mike Mann, as I had been heavily involved as a commuter student during my two years at Miami Dade Community College. I didn't have any generational privilege from a financial standpoint, but I had a once-in-a-lifetime opportunity to attend a prestigious, world-class university, and I was determined to make the most of it.

Because I was a transfer student and had completed all of my general education courses, I entered UM as a junior and had to declare a major before starting classes. I reviewed the list of offered majors and quickly narrowed down my options. I wasn't interested in studying anything too specific; instead, I wanted to focus my time and effort on something that would allow me the flexibility to navigate the business world without being pigeonholed in any one department or area. I also wanted to make sure that whatever major I chose would have a positive return on investment. In the end, I settled on marketing. It had the flexibility I was looking for, and I reasoned that even if I didn't end up working in marketing, at least I'd gain the knowledge I'd need to market myself. Life, after all, is all about marketing.

My first day on the UM campus as a student was very emotional. I clearly remember the moments leading up to my first class. It was an experience I'll never forget. The way the room was set up, the sound of other students mingling, and even the smell of the room was surreal. Sitting at a desk wearing a UM School of Business t-shirt and shorts, I felt overcome with emotion when the professor walked into the room and greeted us. That was the moment that being a student at the University of Miami became real for me. It was the culmination of all the sacrifices my family had made. I felt a strong connection to the two generations of my family who had worked so hard, sacrificed so much, and endured their fair share of immigrant challenges to make it possible for me to be sitting in that seat at that very moment. Their example and encouragement to never quit had taught me that anything is possible if you're willing to work for it. We were all proof of that. I thought of my grandfather who had worked in a factory to provide for his family and all he had sacrificed to bring our family to the United States. I contemplated my father working a blue-collar job despite his excellent management abilities. I was grateful for my mother's devotion to and determination at being the best mother and wife she could possibly be and for providing a peaceful and stable home for us. I thought of my uncle Rolando, who had to take college courses multiple times when he first moved to the United States because he was still learning English and struggled to understand the curriculum well. As I sat there and looked around, some of my privileged classmates might have taken their education for granted, but I most certainly did not.

I think it's important to acknowledge that college isn't only about academics. It's a time of learning and growth as students transition from adolescence to adulthood. During my sophomore year at Miami Dade Community College, while playing trumpet for the University of Miami Marching Band, I met a cute girl named Jennifer McBride. She had beautiful green eyes and was in the Color Guard. Although we were in the band together, we weren't very fond of each other at first. She was a year behind me in school, and I thought she was a little immature. She, on the other hand, thought I was a bit of a snob because I once encouraged my friend Herbie to snub her when she stopped our car to say hello to us. We had plans to be somewhere else and we were running late, so I wanted him to stop talking and go. In hindsight, I agree with Jennifer; my actions were indeed rude. I was a childish guy acting like the center of my own universe, which proves I was as immature as I thought she was.

When I transferred to the University of Miami, I convinced my parents to let me live on campus as a way to have the complete college experience. They weren't fond of the American concept of "going away to college," so living a short distance away in the dorms was a compromise they felt comfortable with. As it turned out, Jennifer lived in the same dormitory building I moved into, although we lived on different floors. Several band members lived on my floor, and we typically left our doors open when we were in. It was a casual and open atmosphere, and it was common for friends and dorm mates to mingle in the halls and socialize. Jennifer started coming down to our floor to visit and started hanging out with me more often, and over time, we became very close. Jennifer was very attractive, easy going and our relationship developed naturally; it was such a gradual process that it's hard to pinpoint exactly when we officially started dating.

One day, my good friend Stewart (who was also in the band and my dorm neighbor) walked into my room, looked me straight in the face, and said, "You know, you're going to marry

Jennifer one day."

I was shocked at the unexpected comment and quipped, "Shut up and get out!" pointing to my open dorm room door.

He chuckled, smirked as if he had a crystal ball, and left. I was stunned, but I couldn't stop thinking about what he had said. My prior girlfriends had been Cuban, so dating a Caucasian girl was an unexpected and unplanned change for me, but in that moment, my relationship with Jennifer became real. It was suddenly not simply a casual friendship but a relationship that might have a future, whether I was ready for it or not.

As a young man, I had convinced myself that marriage wouldn't be a good option for me. I wanted to focus on my career, work twenty hours a day, and date whomever I wanted, whenever I wanted, without any obligations or long-term commitments. I wanted to have my own place where I called all the shots, from location to décor. I wanted to control the smallest details of my life without being accountable to anyone for anything. I saw myself as a free bird and was determined to stay that way. One night, however, the topic of marriage came up in a discussion with a couple of friends, and while I was telling them what I thought I wanted, they pushed back on my way of thinking. As my friends encouraged me to contemplate the benefits of a traditional relationship, I began to think about what it would take for me to change my mind and consider marriage. As I began to contemplate the type of woman who would tolerate the lifestyle I had envisioned for myself, I had no choice but to acknowledge that she didn't exist. It was a fantasy.

Looking back, I realize that part of my hesitancy to marry came from my school environment. In my limited experience, I believed Cuban girls had strong opinions on just about everything and imposed their will in relationships by controlling everything their boyfriends did and didn't do, especially among the more modern generation. Of course, what I just described is a stereotype, but my opinions were shaped by my early experiences with the Cuban girls my age, and that type of woman held no appeal to me. Later, as I matured and ventured outside of my Hispanic neighborhood, I also noticed that the non-Cuban women I was surrounded by at the University of Miami (particularly in the School of Business) were highly focused and career oriented. Although I have no problem with professional women (trust me, I happily hire them today), I felt that marrying an equally intense, career-driven woman would be personally disastrous for me and a future family. It would be a union of fire and explosives, so I concluded that it was best that I be the only Type A personality in a relationship. I needed someone who would complement my personality and drive rather than compete with it. I needed to find a *ying* to my *yang* to give me balance and keep me grounded, and I knew that would be difficult.

My guiding relationship examples have always been my parents. I was aware from a very young age of how well they worked together. It was easy to see how committed they were to each other and to understand the reasons behind the decisions they made. I knew their choices were good because I was the recipient and beneficiary of them. I eventually realized that the lifestyle I had envisioned for myself as a single man wasn't one that would likely be fulfilling. I decided that if I did get married, I wanted the type of marriage my parents had. I recognized, however, that their relationship was possible only because they were both willing to sacrifice and work together in everything they did, from raising children to achieving their financial goals. Their main focus, though, was always on the family, never on themselves as individuals. Their roles were different but complementary, and working together, they were able to achieve remarkable things. When I was young, I also noticed that most of my classmates and friends' parents both worked and were rarely home. I saw how parents would hire caretakers to tend to their children and homes while they pursued their demanding careers or worked multiple jobs to make ends meet. Many of my classmates suffered the consequences of absentee parents. I, on the other hand, benefitted from having a hardworking father and a dedicated mother who chose to stay home and commit her time and talents to raising my brother and I. We never strayed in the wrong direction because we were carefully watched. My life might have turned out very differently if not for their careful and constant guidance. From my perspective, what my parents had achieved was an ideal balance, but I felt that my chances of finding a similar balance was likely impossible in the modern world.

As time passed, I began to admire and appreciate Jennifer's natural qualities, particularly her kindness, good heart, and compassion for animals and children. She wanted to be an educator, and I knew she would be a very good one. Her lack of interest in material things was also very intriguing to me. She was extremely easygoing and didn't like conflict. In fact, arguing made her physically ill. She wasn't controlling nor overbearing. She also had a quiet strength that appealed to me very much. If there were activities I liked that she wasn't interested in (such as watching horror movies), she had no problem with my doing those things with friends. I was comfortable with her pursuing her own interests as well. As a couple, we learned how to adjust our interests to make sure there were activities we could enjoy together. She was naturally happy, satisfied with whatever came her way, and genuinely enjoyed being with me. And most important of all, she accepted me as I was. She wanted to be a part of my life but not control it, and she never asked me to give up anything that brought me joy. All of these qualities were really important to me because I had seen so many of my friends and colleagues date women who were toxic and controlling, and when the relationships predictably ended, they were lost, and all of their previous friendships were strained or broken. As I contemplated all of these things, I realized that Jennifer was exactly the kind of woman I wanted and needed in my life. Our personalities were different, and yet we complemented each other perfectly. My perspective on marriage completely changed, and I began to feel hopeful for the future in a way I never had before.

Just as I was exploring a new way forward in my personal life, I was also forging a unique path in school. I learned early in life that there are many paths that can lead you where you want to go. The trick is to not be afraid of the obstacles and challenges that arise along the way, and to recognize that any problem can be overcome if you're willing to put in the work to solve it. This mindset helped me get into the University of Miami, and it's also proven to be helpful in my professional career. The opportunity to forge my own career path came in 1997 during summer break when I started looking for a summer job. My grades were good, and I was determined to get a job at a respected company even though I had limited work experience. It didn't take long to realize that what I was looking for didn't exist through traditional channels, so I had to figure out a different path to get where I wanted to be. I thought the smartest way to get into a company was to go through a temporary employment agency, so that's what I did. I researched and found an agency that had a good reputation with placing people, and during my general interview, I explained that I was looking for a job as an assistant to a senior executive because I aspired to be an executive myself someday. The temp agency director asked me if I was familiar with Word, Excel, and PowerPoint. I had heard of them, of course, but at that time, those programs had been around for only a short time. The truth was that I had very limited experience with them. Nevertheless, I wasn't about to let computer programs hold me back from my goals, so I assured her that my Microsoft Office knowledge wouldn't be a problem. My confidence in myself paid off, and she immediately placed me with a large company that was putting together a billion-dollar proposal to install cellular towers in South America. I was thrilled and rushed home to learn everything I could about Word, Excel, and PowerPoint before work the next morning.

I reported to the office the next day smiling and ready to work. This was the beginning of my professional work life as I was keenly aware of the significance this job would have on my future career. That awareness originated from a conversation I had overheard between my dad and his cousin Miriam. She said that a person's first professional job is extremely important because it sets the trajectory for the rest of their career. For some reason, her words impacted me, and I never forgot them. When I reported for work on that first day, I asked my new boss, Gina, how I could best help her. As part of our initial conversation, I asked her a series of questions that helped me understand how I could outperform those who had held the same position before me. Then, as I became acquainted with the work, I began to see inefficiencies in the process and asked Gina if she would allow me the freedom to explore different ways of doing things. Luckily, Gina took a liking to me and allowed me to redesign the bid preparation process, which helped us complete the billion-dollar bid on time. My two-week temporary assignment turned into a three-month summer job. I had forged a path that was better than most internships being offered at the time. I had landed a real job with real pay and was allowed to work on a significant project. Best of all, when the summer ended, I had work experience and glowing letters of recommendation to build a résumé around.

As with most things in life, however, my time at the University of Miami wasn't without struggle. In many ways, the traditional school environment was very difficult for me. I had trouble concentrating, and reading long books was unbearable, especially in subjects that didn't interest me. I was concerned that I might have a learning disability, so I made an appointment to be tested for ADHD. When I arrived at the testing facility for my appointment, I asked what would happen if the tests came back positive. The examiner explained to me that the school would contact my professors and inform them that I qualified for extra time for tests and assignments to compensate for my disability. I instantly felt nauseous and told the examiner that I would not be going forward with the testing. I apologized, quickly thanked them, and left. I felt as If I had been punched in the gut. I cried as I rushed back to my dorm. I thought of my family and all the sacrifices, hurt, and obstacles they had had to overcome through the years. I felt like getting any accommodations, when my family had received none, would make me a fraud. I didn't want to be the only one in my family to receive any special treatment. I wanted to earn my degree just as everyone else had, even if it meant I had to struggle to get it. To be clear, I know that ADHD is now a well-recognized and common learning disability, and I'm not opposed to special accommodations for students who legitimately qualify for them. I just didn't feel it was right for me to be tested at that time because I had already come so far and was so close to the finish line that I just needed to push through. The struggle to finish school and earn my college degree on my own meant more to me than anything else. I still suspect I have ADHD, but I'll never know for sure because I've never been formally tested. Jennifer, on the other hand, is sure I have it and always laughs with me about it whenever the topic comes up.

My last summer at the University of Miami was in 1998, and just like the previous year, I needed another job to gain more work experience. I revisited my previous strategy and went back to the temp agency I had used the year before. Because of my prior experience and growing résumé, I was assigned to work at a global logistics company that specialized in shipping freight all over the world. Once again, that two-week assignment turned into a summer-long job. During that summer, I successfully designed a bidding department where I put together all the proposals for the vice president of sales. It was invaluable work experience, and because of my efforts, I was offered a full-time position upon graduation a few months later in December.

The personal culmination of my educational experience, however, was leading the University of Miami marching band as Drum Major my junior and senior years. I figured that my leadership abilities and talent with the trumpet had gotten me through middle school, high school, and community college, so I decided to keep it up through my final years at UM. The skills, friendships, and experiences I gained through my participation in the marching band have been priceless to me. I made lifelong friends and established skills and work habits that helped me achieve educational goals that I might not have otherwise attained. In many ways, I learned more about leadership and organizational management by being a member of the marching band than I did from any classes during my entire educational experience. It was through band that I learned how to lead and found the confidence in myself to do so, so being Drum Major for the University of Miami Band of the Hour was the perfect way for me to end my formal education. It was the bow on the box of my incredible college experience that I will cherish for the rest of my life.

There is no doubt that earning a college degree was a major achievement. My having a degree was physical proof that it's possible for an average immigrant student to attend a great university and graduate. It's important for me to recognize that my parents had a massive role in my educational achievements. From a young age, they instilled in me the importance of formal education and always pointed out the socio-economic lifestyle differences between those who were educated and those who were not. My parents were determined that my brother and I receive all the benefits and opportunities available to us as Americans, and receiving a college education was a major part of that opportunity process for them. On graduation day, after I had received my diploma and was sitting waiting for the ceremony to end, my thoughts were a mix of excitement, gratitude, and anticipation for the future. I felt that even though I had done the work to earn my degree, my diploma really belonged to my parents. After all, if my dad had prioritized his college education in Cuba over moving our family to the United States, I would never have had the opportunity to attend the University of Miami and earn a degree myself. As I left the auditorium and was greeted by my family and friends, I walked to my parents and handed them my diploma, saying, "This is for you." Earning a bachelor's degree was a four-year commitment for me, but it was the culmination of more than two decades of work and sacrifice on my parents' part to get me to that point in my life, and I was profoundly grateful.

Upon graduation, when I returned to the logistics company I had worked at a few months previously, I began as their Marketing Manager, responsible for all the traditional marketing aspects of the company, including public relations, bids, and proposals. I grew in that role for several years, and my responsibilities expanded as my department took on more duties and grew into a significant marketing team. During that time, I also had the opportunity to receive instruction as a sales trainer that certified me to train every salesperson in the company on the process of probing to secure a client. It was a time of personal growth and development that culminated when I was asked to redesign and reimagine the company's sales incentive program. It was a difficult task, but I was able to deliver a product that was embraced by corporate management, branch managers, and, most importantly, the sales team. I'm proud to say that the sales program I designed was the first to be embraced by everyone, and it was not only successfully implemented but had a very good run.

The four-year period after graduation was not only a time for professional growth but also a time of profound personal growth. Jennifer graduated from the University of Miami a year after I did with a degree in education. After graduation, she moved back to her mother's home in Texas and accepted a teaching job in the middle of the school year in January. Jennifer and I were discussing our future, including the possibility of her moving back to Florida. Despite the physical distance in our relationship, we quickly realized that we couldn't imagine being apart from each other indefinitely, so I found a new townhome development in Miami (in an area that would later become the City of Doral), and I put a down payment on a unit in its preconstruction phase. Since Jennifer was in Texas and living with her mom, she was able to save her entire salary, and she sent it to me so we could close on the townhouse. By the fall of 2000, Jennifer had secured a job in an elementary school in Miami and began teaching third grade. While I was learning and growing at the logistics company, Jennifer was learning and growing as a teacher. She even went back to school and obtained a Master's degree. It was an exciting, carefree time in our lives. We felt that the world was at our feet, and we enjoyed our time together doing fun things with family and friends and going on regular vacations.

After we had lived together for about a year, however, I began to feel uncomfortable. I knew we had broken with tradition by living together before marriage, and I didn't feel right about it. I knew that Jennifer deserved more from me and our relationship. After all, she had always shown me unconditional love and support, and the feeling that we were meant to be together was as strong as ever. We had had plenty of opportunities to let each other go through the years, but love had prevailed every single time, and I couldn't imagine my life without her. I wanted us to be a family, so in November of 2001, I proposed, and we were married in July the following year.

As it turned out, I was the first of all my close Cuban and Hispanic friends to marry outside of my culture. My family had to adjust to the reality that my wife didn't speak Spanish, and her family had to come to terms with the fact that there was a loud, opinionated Cuban in their family now. Jennifer and I agreed that our future children would be bilingual and would be raised to love and appreciate both family cultures. We decided to emulate the best parts and qualities of our families and incorporate all those elements into our marriage and home.

After we were married, I continued working as the Marketing Manager at the same logistics company I had been with since graduating from UM until one day, about five years after I had started working there, Mayra, the Chief Information Officer, whom I was very good friends with, came into my office for a chat. The company had been developing operational software in Germany, and they needed a project manager to implement it at local branches in the United States. She offered me the job. I didn't know much about Information Technology (IT) and even less about networks and systems, but I did have a very good working relationship with branch managers and was well respected by them, which from her perspective would be key to success. After all, without the cooperation from those who would use it, the program would never work or ever come to fruition. I wasn't sure about the offer, so we agreed that I would sleep on it and get back to her in the morning.

As I weighed my options, I considered my current position. I was very good at my job and enjoyed my work immensely. I was a Marketing Manager, not a Project Manager, and I knew very little about IT—and honestly, I wasn't sure if I was curious enough to know more. It was scary and foreign to me, like arriving as an immigrant in an unknown country. I also knew that if I accepted the new position, the department I had worked so hard to build and develop would be downsized significantly. If I failed at the new position, there would be no going back. Leaving the known for the unknown was risky. I already understood the sales aspect of the company, but I realized that if I accepted this new role, I would be in a unique position to understand all aspects of the company. In addition to sales and marketing, I would gain a deep understanding of air and sea freight, imports and exports, customs clearance, IT, controlling, and accounting. With this knowledge, I would be the only person in the entire organization to have a deep insight of every department and to understand how they all synced together. I understood that knowledge is power, and by accepting the new role, I would once again be forging a new path for myself.

The next morning, Mayra came into my office with her coffee in hand. I looked at her and confidently said, "I'll do it."

She smiled and said, "Exciting!" She turned around and walked out. She went to the president's office to pass on the news, and half an hour later, I was called in. The president was ecstatic and could hardly contain himself because he saw my acceptance of the new role as an opportunity to pawn me off to an IT department in Germany and downsize (or eliminate) the marketing department. The longer he spoke, the more confident I felt that I had made the right decision. When the discussion came to the topic of compensation, he smirked and suggested a performance-based compensation plan. I blurted out a very large number, which he immediately accepted. There was no doubt in my mind that he believed I would fail because the program I would be working on had been in development for years with very little implementation progress to show for it. I can still see the smirk on his face. He was absolutely convinced I would never see any of that money, at least not under his tenure. Little did he know that his lack of faith in me was major motivation for me to succeed, and I wasted no time. I left his office and immediately got to work.

My new job was exciting. I had a lot to learn, but I was eager to understand and solve problems. I started traveling to Germany and established very successful business relationships with my colleagues at the global headquarters. I had teams in Germany and the United States working on the software system's rollout. The work was challenging, but in the end, my team and I were successful, and we rolled the system out on time and without any major delays or complications. I will never forget the email I received from the company president after the owner of the company congratulated me in a global company email after the first module was implemented. He acknowledged that I had been able to do what no one had thought possible. Shortly thereafter, the president was abruptly terminated, but not before he authorized HR to release the first portion of the performance-based compensation plan we had agreed on. I was elated. I knew I had achieved something unexpected, which motivated me to work even harder to do it again.

As I experienced consistent success in my new role, I began to be regularly promoted. Not surprisingly, the snide president was let go, and a new president and CEO was installed. Unlike his predecessor, the new president was intelligent, supportive, respectful, and fun to work with. We quickly bonded, and he learned to rely on my knowledge of systems to help him make good decisions.

After my success with implementing the new system in the United States, I was tasked with implementing system rollouts in Canada and afterwards throughout South America. As these rollouts continued, I identified operational inefficiencies and redesigned bad business processes. In this manner, we were able to put in place standardized operating practices that optimized operations throughout the regions. Within two years of accepting my new role, I was promoted and became the youngest director for a worldwide company with over fifteen thousand employees. I was a prominent senior management team member responsible for both North and South America and was specifically advising company presidents across continents on how to run their local operations in compliance with the standards we were setting. I was only twenty-seven years old and light-years ahead of my peers.

And yet, despite my corporate success, I began to feel

dissatisfied. I was tired of working under individuals who had the ability to cut me or my team as they wished. I had also worked under five company presidents but had had good working relationships with only three of them (with the last being the worst of all). I was proud of all I had accomplished, but I had a desire to build something myself, so in addition to my full-time job, I started a fertilization and pest control franchise business with my neighbor José. My father had worked two jobs for several years, so I figured I could do the same.

We structured the business so that José would do the day work and I would run the administrative part of the business in the evenings. Unfortunately, there were challenges right from the start. José was financially undisciplined and stubborn, and he had a hard time seeing the big picture when it came to business. Once while fertilizing, José burned a client's entire lawn. The customer was justifiably upset and asked to speak to a manager. José called me in a panic, so I took time out of my day to meet with the client. When I got there, I listened carefully to the client's concerns and determined the cause of the problem. During the course of our conversation, he asked me about my day job, and after we spoke for a while, he offered to introduce me to an acquaintance who ran a public logistics company. I agreed, and a week later, I was hired as Executive Vice President and Chief Operating Officer of the company, making nearly double what I had been earning. Changing jobs was a risk, but Jennifer was about to have our first child, and I felt I needed to do everything I could to make sure I was providing for our family. With the increase in my income, we wouldn't have to rely on Jennifer's salary, and she would be able to stay home for the first few years of our child's life. It was an opportunity I couldn't pass up.

When I tendered my resignation at the company I had worked at for almost a decade, everyone was surprised. The news went all the way up to the owners, and they did all they could to persuade me to stay, but in the end, my new salary as an Executive Vice President was more than they were paying their Vice Presidents, so they weren't willing to make a counteroffer. I'll always be grateful for the time I spent at that company, though. I started my full-time employment with them right after graduating from college and had experienced remarkable personal and professional growth there. I was thankful for the opportunities and will always cherish the friendships I made there, but it was time to move on and start a new chapter in my professional life.

CHAPTER 5

A Time of Growth

"America is 'one nation under God,' and if we're humble enough to acknowledge that and apply a sense of gratitude in all we do, the path to achieving our American Dream is not only possible, but inevitable."

I started work at the new logistics company in May 2007, and a week later, our son, Noah, was born. I came into the new job full of energy and optimism, but within five days of working there, I realized that something was seriously wrong. The business model was good and had a lot of potential for growth, but the methods used to make and spend money were not. For example, if the company made $5 million in revenue, the chairman would spend $30 million in marketing campaigns to promote the stock, not the product. It was all about public relations. The focus was not on healthy business practices but on finding ways to move the stock, even if only slightly. The chairman was also vehemently against the Securities and Exchange Commission

(SEC), which I thought was very strange. I had worked there for only about four months when the SEC came in, put the company under receivership, and shut down operations. More than fifty employees were laid off without warning and simply sent home without severance packages or final paychecks.

The situation was shocking. I should have felt panicked, but I was so worried for my coworkers that I barely had time to think of myself. We were a single-income family with a newborn, but I remember thinking that just as this opportunity had come to me, a new path would soon reveal itself. And that's exactly what happened. Before being shut down by the government, the company had been in the process of trying to purchase a private aviation company owned by Michael McCauley. During my four-month tenure at the company, I had established a close personal relationship with Michael and had developed a personal interest in the aviation business generally. When the logistics company went into receivership, Michael immediately hired me as a consultant and then later as his Executive Vice President. I worked for Michael at his aviation company for two years, where I learned the aviation business and even sold an airplane. Everything was new to me, but I didn't let that intimidate me or slow me down. Just as with every other job I'd had, I threw myself into it and adapted my skills to the work. After two years of working for Michael, however, I began to feel unfulfilled. Michael was paying me handsomely for my advice, but I no longer felt he was listening to me. The situation culminated when I wanted to terminate an employee whom I felt was hurting the company and taking advantage of Michael's goodwill and generosity. Michael didn't see the situation the same way I did and insisted on trusting the individual because he had been a good asset to the company in the past. Once my ideas and suggestions weren't being considered, I knew it was time to go, so I resigned. Michael was shocked by my decision, but he accepted my resignation, and most importantly, we remained friends. Unfortunately, it turned out that I was right about the individual I wanted to terminate.

When I left Michael's aviation company in 2009, I decided it was time for me to be my own boss. I was done working for other individuals, so I decided to forge a new path for myself. I learned about an investment opportunity in a gold mine in Brazil through some family friends that really intrigued me. The man who allegedly owned the land was Brazilian. He was extremely charismatic, carried himself well, and appeared to be wealthy. He had all the proper documents to substantiate his ownership of the land, and the people surrounding him brought a sense of credibility and assurance to his claims. A neighboring plot of land was already being used as a successful, producing mine, and the studies showed that "our" mine had the potential to produce even more—potentially more than $1 billion (USD). The land had never been touched, so the idea was to raise funds to get equipment to the site and start operating as soon as possible. I was comfortable with everyone involved, had done my due diligence, and felt that it was a safe (albeit unconventional) bet. In fact, I felt so strongly about the project and the prospect of commodity trading that I encouraged family members to invest in the mine as well. I wanted everyone to do as well with the investment as I expected to.

When we began the project, I felt a high level of confidence, but it didn't take long before I noticed that the Brazilian began to shift his focus from the mine to other projects. Millions of dollars were coming in from investors, but the funds weren't being used for their intended purpose. I had no idea where the money was going, but after several months, it was obvious to me that the project was failing, and the pressure was on. I kept my cool outwardly, but inside I was terrified. I couldn't believe that I had gotten it so terribly wrong, and the reality that I could lose everything was sinking in. If it had been only my own money that was invested, I could have coped more easily, but I felt financially accountable and morally responsible for the money my family had invested. I still believe today that the venture might have been a spectacular success if the funds hadn't been misappropriated, and interestingly, the man managing the venture eventually served time in prison for his participation in a different investment scheme that wasn't run properly.

I spent two years pursing the Brazilian businessman, trying to recoup the investments I had entrusted him with before I realized it was time to give up and move on. Those two years were a very difficult and dark time in my life. I went from being professionally and financially successful to being unemployed and at my lowest point having only $367 in my checking account. Up to that point, my career had been steadily progressing, and

I had felt good about what I had accomplished, but it all felt invalidated by this colossal failure, and it was difficult for me to accept. Two years might seem like a long time to chase broken promises, but I owed my father and uncle an astronomical amount of money, and I felt a deep moral obligation to recover the funds and pay them back no matter how long it took.

When I finally accepted that the venture was failing, and with bankruptcy looming on the horizon, I flew to Los Angeles one last time to meet with the Brazilian. On the flight there, I read a book on how banks and lending institutions worked in relation to mortgages, credit cards, and debt collection. I did everything I could to understand the realities of the situation I was in, and then, just as my parents had done so many years ago, I devised a bold plan to eliminate my debt, clean my financial record, and rebuild my life. I began by selling three investment properties for a loss during the height of the global Great Recession that began in December 2007 and lasted through June 2009. I also drained my 401k to have money to live off of while I worked to recover our investments. I had almost $150,000 saved in my 401k by the time I was thirty years old. It was terrible taking all the money out, having to pay the early withdrawal penalty fees, and, worst of all, missing out on what would have grown into a solid long-term investment. Nevertheless, it was a crucial step in our financial survival and had to be done.

By shifting assets around and living off savings, I managed to keep our home and avoid going into bankruptcy. And yet, despite my own worries, the most painful and stressful aspect of the situation was the realization that my parents and uncle had lost a significant amount of money to the failed venture. It was unbearable for me. They were disappointed in the failure, of course, but they also worried about how devastated I was with the entire situation. As I worked to regain our investments, I gave them regular updates, and it was always embarrassing to report the broken promises and false hopes given by the Brazilian. However, I can honestly say that, second only to my wife, it was my family's love and support that carried me through that terrible time. In a strange way, their patience, kindness, and understanding made me even more committed (if that were possible) to making them whole.

And then, amid all of the chaos and stress, Jennifer and I welcomed our second son, Evan, into our family. He was a ray of light and happiness in an otherwise dark and concerning time. Through it all, I did my best to show my family confidence and strength. I carried my worries deep inside, and although Jennifer understood what I was going through, she carried the burden and responsibility of caring for a toddler and an infant while keeping the household running. Even though our situation was precarious, I never asked or wanted Jennifer to go back to work. I valued the role she played as a full-time mother, and I figured that if my parents had been able to sacrifice so my mom could stay home and raise my brother and I, that was the least I could do for my own children.

Finally, on a warm evening in August 2011, after two years doing all I could to retrieve the gold mine investments without success and barely managing to survive financially, I went for a walk and decided to call Michael McCauley. Michael and I had maintained a friendship after I'd left his aviation company, so he was aware of my situation. In the days preceding the call, I prayed to find a new path, so after much thought and meditation, I asked him if there was an opportunity for us to work together again. Not only did I need a steady income, I also needed reliable health insurance for my young family. Without hesitation, Michael replied, "Absolutely. Come tomorrow!" I felt immediate relief and gratitude. It was as if I had been floating on a raft in the middle of the ocean and suddenly a boat appeared to rescue me. After two years chasing broken promises and losing everything except the relationships that mattered most to me, it was time to get back to work and close the gold mine chapter of my life once and for all.

Looking back, I learned several invaluable lessons from that painful, heart-wrenching experience. First, I learned exactly how strong I am. When faced with overwhelming trials, it's easy to give up or try to find an easy way out, but maintaining my integrity was massive motivation for me, and I was committed to never giving up. I was determined to do all I could to restore the trust and confidence my family had placed in me. I realized that I'd have to work harder than ever before to plug the giant financial hole I had made. Maybe if I hadn't lost any money I wouldn't have worked so hard, but attaching a monetary figure to my failure motivated me to come back stronger than ever. I also vowed to never put myself in a similar situation again and, more specifically, to never raise money for other people again.

An important factor in how I was able to navigate this period in my life was the quiet and constant support of my wife. While I was gone trying to recoup funds, Jennifer was focused on providing a loving and stable home for our family. Every time I came home empty-handed, she never criticized me or made me feel like a failure in any way. Her confidence in me and her unwavering support allowed me to stay calm even when it felt as if the world were collapsing around us. Jennifer knows me well, so she understands that no one is harder on me than I am. To this day, she occasionally reminds me that I expect too much perfection in all I do and encourages me to loosen up and gain perspective in her quiet, subtle way. She is the perfect counterbalance to me, and without her support, I don't think I would have made it through that time. I also think it's generally true that when couples go through very difficult periods of life, they either grow through it together or grow apart. I'm proud to say that we survived and grew even closer through that phase of our lives.

When I went back to work with Michael, I wasn't exactly sure what I would be doing. I knew I didn't want to work for him as an employee but rather as a partner, even if that meant we worked on different ventures. Michael agreed, and I immediately began looking for opportunities. I made it a habit to monitor Michael's emails because he wasn't particularly good at keeping up with them and he granted me access to sort through them. I wanted to help him, and I figured that buried in those hundreds and thousands 'of emails, an unnoticed opportunity could be sitting there waiting to be plucked. Sure enough, an American expat living in China had reached out to several US aviation operators looking for a company he could represent oversees. I sensed that this could be exactly the business situation I was looking for, so I responded and opened a dialogue. After several weeks of communicating and building a relationship of trust with my contact, I decided to get on a plane and visit him in Shanghai to determine if this was an opportunity worth pursuing. When I got there, I could instantly see that there was plenty of opportunity for growth in China, so I hired the American expat and immediately began pitching my market penetration strategy to some key players. It was a risky move because I don't speak Mandarin and knew very little about Chinese culture, but I knew I had the business knowledge and American industry experience to find, promote, and create a niche of aviation services to growing companies in China.

After several months of discussions and negotiations with the largest aircraft operator in China at the time, I was entrusted with two BBJs (737s with a stateroom inside) and an ACJ (an Airbus version of the Boeing 737). If I had told anyone in the industry that I had gone to China and had taken delivery of three $80 million aircraft without a single investor and very little capital, they would have never believed it. Needless to say, landing the contract was a major boost to my morale and confidence, especially after the gold mine fiasco, and I was incredibly grateful for the opportunity to prove myself again and be in a partnership where I provided value. The takeaway from all this is that a good idea is a good idea, and fortunately for me, I had the business knowledge and confidence to bring people together to make it happen.

The China deal put me on the aviation industry map, and as more opportunities opened up, I cultivated as many as I could. Of course, there have been hardships and challenges along the way for both Michael and I, but despite the challenges, opportunities have always followed them like a rainbow after a storm. My story in the aviation industry is not over, but I've held several successful President and CEO positions and have been part of acquiring multiple companies alongside my partners. During the Covid-19 pandemic, while many businesses were failing, we were growing our aviation portfolio serving niche markets with very limited competition. For one of our ventures, I led the acquisition of a foreign airline operator that we turned into a massive cargo operation. We also acquired a second airline with a maintenance facility that had been losing money for over a decade and, within the first month, turned a profit and have continued to do so. At the time of writing this book, we have as a group exceeded $500 million (USD) in sales, and I can clearly see the pathway forward for us to reach $1 billion (USD) in revenue in a fraction of the time it took us to get to this point.

I would also like to acknowledge that Jennifer and I have been successful in our marriage as well. All relationships are difficult at times and require constant maintenance, but so far, I'd say that marriage to Jennifer has been relatively easy. We may not be perfect, but we are perfect for each other and balance each other out. Like my parents, we make a great team, and I could never have achieved what I have professionally if it weren't for her unwavering support. I spend a lot of time traveling for work, but I'm able to do so only because I know Jennifer is home with the kids, giving them a well-managed and stable home full of love, structure, and support. When I'm home, I focus on being present for Jennifer and the boys. We travel together as a family and take nothing for granted as we've learned firsthand that everything can be gone in a moment. We've also learned that the key to happiness is to express gratitude for all of our blessings, big and small. As long as we have a life full of joy and love, everything else is a bonus.

And yet, despite all the monetary success and professional accolades, I still see myself as an average immigrant kid striving to achieve the American Dream. I know I'm not better, smarter, or luckier than anyone else, but I think I'm more determined and focused on the vision I have for my life than most people, and I work hard every day to make that vision a reality. I also strive to see the positives in every situation, even when things seem bleak. I feel incredibly blessed to have the opportunity to pursue my dreams in the greatest nation on Earth, and I thank God for all that I am and for all that I have. America is indeed "one nation under God," and if we're humble enough to acknowledge that and apply a sense of gratitude in all we do, the path to achieving our American Dream is not only possible but inevitable.

CHAPTER 6

Dear America

"No one knows what they have until they lose it."

If you want to really know someone and understand why they think the way they do, it's essential you know their story. The way we think and what we believe are largely shaped by our experiences. This book was written in 2021, in the time directly following the initial Covid-19 pandemic and shutdowns. It has been a time of civil unrest, political obsession, and social upheaval. It's been a time of doubt and uncertainty regarding freedom and personal responsibility. Now that you know my story, you shouldn't be surprised when I unequivocally say that America is by far the greatest country on Earth. As an immigrant and a person who has traveled extensively and witnessed the realities of the world, I can think of nothing more insulting or perplexing than to witness hatred for our country coming from within. America is the greatest socioeconomic experiment ever conducted and has been wildly successful, and not just for Americans, but for the entire world. Of course, there have been mistakes and difficulties throughout our history, but by and large, American exceptionalism, embodied by "we the people," has prevailed through it all.

My parents had a saying they liked to tell my brother and me growing up: "No one knows what they have until they lose it." There is great truth in that statement, especially when considering all that America has to offer. We are sitting at the brink of a precipice. There are those who want to fundamentally change America, from the Constitution to the way we live and the choices we are allowed to make on an individual level. On the other hand, there are those of us who are fighting to preserve the timeless principles of the Constitution. We want to affirm that this country still offers the best hope for freedom and personal prosperity; however, that can be achieved only by keeping the promise of America alive. In recent years, a powerful few have not only embraced but are actively promoting socialism. They are working to convince ordinary Americans that our political system, which has done so much for so many, is "rigged" and benefits only a favored few. This disingenuous political tactic has destroyed many once-great nations, and we must not let that happen to America. Unlike past threats to our way of life and overall freedoms that have come from outside of our borders, America's most dangerous enemies now come from within. Destructive ideologies are being embedded within our society to systematically undermine and transform the essence of what makes America special and unique. We can't learn our lesson after America is lost. We must do all we can to learn from other fallen nations if we are to prevent our own national demise.

The following chapters are my thoughts on issues we are confronting as a nation today. It is my hope that perhaps something I share might help you think from a different perspective and consider a new approach to the topics being discussed today. We have a nation to save, and I would like nothing more than for you and me to do it together.

CHAPTER 7

C Student to CEO

*"A C student can be CEO and achieve extreme success
if you set your mind to it!"*

The major emphasis of school, at any level, has historically been on grades and standardized tests. That was certainly the case when I started school in the 1980s, and it's still true today. The public school system, together with parents, places a disproportionate amount of energy on students getting good grades as the sole definer of scholastic worth. Although there's nothing wrong with getting good grades and excelling academically, there will always be students who fall short of the ideal. These students may be struggling with learning disabilities or have extremely difficult home lives, or perhaps they're more interested in working with their hands rather than learning from books. Whatever the case, a high GPA on its own is an inadequate predictor of whether a child will be financially successful in life.

Most people I interact with assume I was great at school because of what I've been able to accomplish professionally. The reality is that I felt inept with schooling when I was growing up. I hated school and generally didn't get As. No matter how many times I committed to doing better, it just never happened. I never thought I was as smart or would ever be as successful as those who had high GPAs and excellent SAT scores. What came so easily to others was very difficult for me, and I realized that it would be extremely difficult to get good grades, so I inevitably gave up along the way.

As I struggled through school and moved into my college years, I had an epiphany and began to see my situation differently. I realized that most of those who were truly academically gifted (we often call them "book smart") actually lacked a lot skills and abilities in other areas, and ironically, many were the least rounded people I knew. Although they had the ability to read and process abstract information quickly, they also seemed to struggle to connect with other people. Many also had a false sense of confidence. They had been told their entire lives that they were exceptional; had received numerous accolades, awards, and recognitions; and had succeeded in all of their school endeavors. Many felt superior to those they viewed as less intelligent because they were acing everything. But were they?

It's been my professional experience that extremely academically gifted people seem to struggle as they move out of a school system and transition into the work field (what we commonly refer to as "the real world"). Of course, this is not true in every situation or profession, but it happens often enough that we can make some generalizations, especially in business settings where entrepreneurship, interpersonal skills, and creativity are vital to success. High academic achievers often struggle working with others, especially in leadership roles that are awarded on skill set and character traits rather than on test scores alone. Taking direction from someone who has vision and charisma but no scholastic pedigree can be difficult for them to accept. They also sometimes have a difficult time creating rapport with those who are more outgoing and open and not as "book smart." The reality is that once you exit the academic environment, the skills you needed to get incredibly good grades are not the skills you necessarily need to get promotions and build an impressive résumé, team, and career. The playing field completely changes, and high academic achievers begin at the same starting line as everyone else. You might have gotten straight A's in science, math, and English courses but be incapable of keeping a client satisfied with the product or service you're providing. The C student, on the other hand, may have an easier time interacting with clients because of the skills they cultivated by talking during class (instead of paying attention), being social (instead of staying home studying), and having fun with friends (instead of working extensively on special projects).

I happen to be one of those students who went from being a C student and a horrible test-taker to a successful businessman, and I believe anyone in the same situation can do it too. Never forget that you don't have to be an amazing scholar to succeed; you just have to understand how to assemble and utilize the skills and talents of the people you work with. For example, whenever I assemble a team, I avoid overly zealous intellectuals, especially if they are negative and incapable of working in a group. Instead I look for people who have a strong work ethic and a sense of humility, and who will work hard to make the group succeed without needing constant praise and validation. I also look for a mix of personalities and traits because, in the end, it's a good idea to have a variety of approaches to and perspectives on solving problems. By choosing a diverse group, I can then use my strengths to help propel the group forward, and any weaknesses that I have can be bolstered by the group's collective strengths. These are some of the things that are not taught in a classroom and can be learned only in real life. If you feel inferior because of a perceived lack of education or academic prowess, let me make something clear: as long as you look the part, communicate well, and have a strategic perspective on achieving success, you will most likely go further than those who rely on their school credentials to get ahead.

To be successful, you not only need technical knowledge, but you also need to understand workplace politics and how to navigate through those situations successfully. To be successful, you must be insightful, full of energy, charming, and know how to lead without being despised. You may have all of the necessary qualities, but if you can't sell your ideas, they're worth nothing.

You might have the best ideas and strategies to move forward, but if your team and superiors aren't on your side, and if you fail to win them over, you're finished before you even started. These are skill sets that aren't taught in a classroom, and you either have them or you don't. All of a sudden, being the person with the best grades in the room is not necessarily an advantage and could actually be a detriment if not handled carefully. Once you are out of the school environment, straight A's mean very little if you don't have the ability to make new things happen.

I want to be clear that my thoughts here are generalized. I know many people who did very well in school and have also succeeded, and I think it's important to note that there's a big difference between cumulative grades and grades earned in a particular subject matter. I think we can all agree that a surgeon needs to have high grades and technical skills to prove mastery before being certified to perform surgery; however, knowing whether that doctor earned an A in accounting, English, or art is not as relevant. So we must keep it all in perspective.

When planning for your future, keep in mind that career success is determined mainly by how hard you're willing to work and not necessarily on high academic performance in school. You don't need to be a valedictorian to be successful in life; you just need to have a goal and be willing to work harder than everyone else to achieve it. It's also essential to understand that there are many paths to get where you want to be. College is one path, but it may not necessarily be the right path for you. Carefully consider all of your options, and don't be afraid to choose the path that's best for you and your life, even if it's unconventional.

My advice to anyone thinking of going to college would be to get a good education anywhere you can. You don't have to attend an overpriced, top-rated school to be successful. Every school has its own set of very successful graduates. While you're in school, work hard and do your best, but don't worry if you're not the best student in every subject or whether you get an A in every class. You can learn valuable lessons in any classroom or situation you find yourself in. Wherever you go and whatever your abilities may be, commit to being the hardest-working person in the room. Focus on polishing your communication skills: become a good writer, and learn to speak in a proper, well-mannered way. Fine-tune your ability to problem-solve, and keep yourself under control at all times. When you leave college and enter the workforce, never stop learning. The more experience you have in your field, the less your college degree matters and the more valuable your experience becomes. Take it from me: a C-student can be CEO and achieve extreme success if they set their mind to it, prove themselves, and become an expert in their field.

CHAPTER 8

Cancel Culture

"The only thing that should be cancelled is cancel culture itself."

Amerrica is a nation built on Judeo-Christian values. We were taught and understand that people often fall short of the ideal in many ways, but we believe in forgiveness, especially when the repentance offered is real and sincere. These values kept us moving in the right direction for generations . . . until recently. In the past sixty years, there has been an unmistakable shift in attitude towards traditional Judeo-Christian values. What was once revered is now mocked and scorned as the trend is now toward atheism and the glorification of the self over God. We have moved away from religion as a society, and because we have lost our religious guiding principles, what we are left with is rage. The process of seeking and granting forgiveness is what makes us and our society good, but the trend now is to ban, shun, and cancel transgressors. Mercy is nowhere to be found. This is extremely troubling because no real or meaningful progress can ever be made, as individuals or as a society, without repentance and forgiveness.

The new phenomena of "cancel culture" being pushed on society today is extremely concerning. Cancel culture is a modern form of ostracism in which an individual or organization is thrust out of social or professional circles, whether it be online, on social media, or in person. Those subjected to this form of ostracism are said to have been "cancelled." Although it is useful for a society to call out inappropriate and dangerous language or behaviors, cancel culture as we know it goes against everything we stand for as a Judeo-Christian society. Cancel culture is a hypocritical movement used as a weapon to excise those in opposition to woke, trendy values, especially if those individuals espouse conservative political viewpoints. It is misguided virtue signaling whereby the same standards do not apply to all. Cancel culture is vigilantism and runs counter to the governing principle of our justice system whereby the accused are innocent until proven guilty. Sadly, the cancel culture mob is directed by small groups of people who are intent to ruin as many lives as possible simply because they have differing views from theirs. It goes against everything we stand for as a nation and as fair-minded individuals. Cancel culture is a dangerous and insincere practice that erodes societal norms and turns Americans against each other. How did we get to this point, and what can we do about it?

One of the many insidious problems with cancel culture is that it's not applied evenly. For example, if we wanted to cancel everyone who has ties to racism, the Democratic Party wouldn't exist. The reality is that the Democratic Party has deep ties to slavery, racist Jim Crow laws in the South, and public political support of segregation laws. Another interesting comparison can be made with blackface. According to the Merriam-Webster dictionary, blackface refers to the practice of wearing dark makeup to "mimic the appearance of a Black person and especially to mock or ridicule Black people. The wearing of blackface by white performers was, from the early nineteenth through the mid-twentieth centuries, a prominent feature of minstrel shows and similar forms of entertainment featuring exaggerated and inaccurate caricatures of Black people." The use of blackface is now considered to be a deeply offensive and a racist practice.

On October 23, 2018, NBC host Megyn Kelly came under fire for participating in a discussion in regard to darkening skin for Halloween costumes. Kelly pointed out that when she was young, it wasn't uncommon for a person to darken their skin if they were dressing up as a black character for Halloween (she used the example of Diana Ross). It was, in her opinion, a way of paying tribute to black celebrities, actors, singers, or sports stars. Kelly immediately came under fire for her comments, and although she offered a heartfelt apology, she was fired from NBC three days later. Keep in mind that Kelly was fired for engaging in a discussion of blackface, not for wearing blackface.

Now let's consider Ralph Northam. In February of 2019,

less than six months after Megyn Kelly was fired from NBC, Ralph Northam, the Democratic governor of Virginia, admitted to dressing in a racist manner that was documented in a picture in his 1984 medical school yearbook. The photo depicts one individual dressed as a minstrel in blackface standing closely to another individual dressed in the robes of the Ku Klux Klan. The photo, by anyone's standards, is undoubtedly racist, and although Northam admitted to being in the picture, he refused to specify which costume he was dressed in. Usually a person in Governor Northam's situation would be immediately cancelled from politics, fired, or professionally censored. Unbelievably, none of this happened to Northam. Although there was significant pressure for him to resign, Northam apologized and held his ground, and the cancel culture mob eventually moved on and later praised Northam for "doing the work," whatever that means.

Compare Ralph Northam's experience with Megyn Kelly's. Megyn Kelly had formerly worked for Fox News, a conservative news network, and therefore could be shown no mercy, while Ralph Northam was a Democratic governor in the state of Virginia. This is just one of numerous examples of how people are specifically targeted and harassed by the cancel culture mob if you represent conservative values while their liberal counterparts may be subject only to mild criticism and ultimately redemption.

It has become clear over the past couple of years that the left despises people who think differently from them. Their anger and rage consume them, and they lash out at any conservative or moderate individual who gains power or notoriety in order to silence them and limit their ability to spread their ideas. In contrast, conservatives detest bad ideas, but they are willing to engage in conversations surrounding their ideology. It's difficult, however, to communicate from extremes, and when two parties are unable or unwilling to engage in civilized conversation, what we are left with is censorship to curtail speech. This is fundamentally anti-American, and the evidence suggests that social media giants such as Facebook and Twitter, the mainstream media, public education, and fringe political groups such as Antifa and BLM share the vast majority of the blame.

The main problem with cancel culture is that it does not allow for mistakes, repentance, and growth. Everyone makes mistakes or says foolish things they regret. That's part of the evolution of the self and used to be understood and accepted as part of the process of maturing. The advent of social media, however, has changed the metric by which we judge people. Now we have the ability to go back ten years or more and find damning pictures or insensitive comments made by a person when they were in high school. I think we can all agree that teenagers often say and do things that are in poor taste, but that's more an indication of their age and immaturity than their character. The teenage years are a time of rapid growth and learning, and assigning permanent repercussions to comments made during this time is cruel. Haven't we all said and done things during our teenage years that we regret? Why can't we forgive and ensure young adults learn from their mistakes and become better people? After all, if perfection is the standard, then we all fall short, no matter our age.

In Cuba and other Communist countries throughout the world, the government has control over all aspects of life. They control the media, commerce, schools, etc. A person who doesn't embrace Communist values gets cancelled too. A cancelled person in Cuba can't get food, supplies, or a job, or have any basic standing in society. When my father wanted to get married in a church, he was warned that he was at risk of losing his job and being sent to an internment camp to "realign his thoughts and commitment to the one party that mattered." Thankfully that didn't happen, but how is my father's experience different from what is happening in America today? Cancel culture is a tool to silence people and not allow them to express their opinion. The threat may be implied or real, but either way, the obvious outcome to this type of oppression is for individuals to go silent, which is exactly what's happening. Most conservatives, independents, and other like-minded groups with conservative leanings are choosing to keep their thoughts and opinions to themselves. This is one reason that polling over the last decade has been so unreliable. It's all very un-American and reminds me of the secret conversations whispered at Cuban dinner tables at the beginning of the revolution.

My point in sharing my family's experiences is not necessarily to educate about life in Cuba but rather to provide a contrast so we can examine life in America more closely. Do you see any parallels? Are there Communist-like tendencies creeping into American society under the guise of equality and fairness? One of the dangers of being an American in 2022 is that many don't understand history and are enamored with theories and ideologies that have failed consistently in the past. Americans are blinded by code words that sound and feel good without having firsthand knowledge of their implications. It's human nature to think the grass is greener on the other side, but having come from the other side, I can assure you we must keep our American values intact. If we don't, we will one day wake up in a country we don't recognize, having become the oppressive country many of us have sacrificed all to flee from.

We need to make sure that in America, everyone can continue to speak freely regardless of their political views. Topics should be honestly and vigorously debated without censorship or fear of reprisal. We should be united in purpose and principle, not divided by subjective opinion. And most of all, we need to put an end to cancel culture before it destroys our society. The end result of cancel culture is an America deeply divided. Conservative people will move to conservative states where they can speak freely and live among other like-minded individuals. The silent majority will begin to buy products only from conservative-run companies and boycott stores and companies who mock and belittle their political and religious beliefs. For the record, I disagree with this approach; however, it seems to be the obvious outcome if we don't start an immediate course correction. This is the true danger of cancel culture. It pits us against each other, and the result will be devastating because while there are laws to prevent discrimination against sex, race, gender, etc., there is not a law in place preventing discrimination against an individual based on political belief or affiliation.

We need to start identifying as Americans *first*, ahead of race, gender, or political preference. In order for our system to work, we need to recommit to honoring the values and freedoms guaranteed to United States citizens in the Constitution. America is the most charitable nation on earth, and whenever we experience a challenge or misfortune, no other country comes together as we do. We do not cancel each other in times of need or despair. Consider Pearl Harbor, September 11th, or even the tragic collapse of a Miami Beach condominium. We all come together in times of need and become Americans first. We cannot allow small fringe groups to cancel American values. We need to defend America and what she stands for. Labeling America as an oppressor or claiming it's a terrible place is not only disingenuous but dangerous as well. After all, if the United States were as horrible as the left claims it is, why are there so many people around the world trying to come here? The silent majority needs to find their voice to protect and save America from those who are trying to destroy it. Blocking, physically assaulting, shaming, and ostracizing are behaviors that should not be tolerated in a free and civilized society.

My family escaped Cuba to be able to speak their mind freely. They sacrificed everything they had to enjoy the freedoms many Americans take for granted today. That means that sometimes we will get it wrong before we get it right. It also means having the compassion and humility to not only admit when we are wrong, but also having the willingness to forgive those who have wronged us. We need to resist the urge to control speech to ensure that opposing views will never be heard. Many countries have lost their way, but we must not let that happen here in America. We must not let history repeat itself. The only thing that should be cancelled is cancel culture itself.

CHAPTER 9

Choose Your Circle

"Tell me who you spend time with and I'll tell you who you are!"

It was my privilege to be raised in a loving and stable home. While my dad worked hard to provide for the financial needs of our family, my mom dedicated her life to being at home and raising my brother and I. My mom was beautiful, kind, and compassionate. She treated my brother and I like precious gifts, and I trusted her completely. I knew instinctively that she wanted the very best for me, and she would do all she could to help me grow and develop into a good man. She carefully guided me as I matured, and one thing she routinely said altered the course of my life. She said, "Tell me who you spend time with and I'll tell you who you are." At first this saying really bothered me. It felt judgmental, and I wanted to be carefree and accepted by

97

everyone. Nevertheless, as with all things my parents taught me, this saying impacted me and became a part of my subconscious. When I left my parents' home and ventured out into the world on my own, my mother's saying stayed with me. Later, as I watched the people around me succeed or fail, I couldn't help but notice how their circle of friends influenced them and affected their outcome. Unsurprisingly, it turns out my mother was right.

As with all truth, my mother's words of wisdom weren't limited to just my brother and I, but can be applied to everyone in nearly all stages of life. The people we choose to spend our time with can have a significant impact on our lives. For example, what teachers do you choose to listen to? Whom do you turn to for advice? What job will be best for you? Which movies and television shows do you choose to watch? Which gym, club, networking circle, or social clubs do you choose to join? What church do you belong to? What books do you read? The people, organizations, and things we associate with on a daily basis form our world and the type of person we become.

I think it's fair to acknowledge that the world is full of unique individuals from all walks of life. No two people will interact with the world in exactly the same manner, and we will all make mistakes along the way. Without struggle, failures, challenges, heartache, and disappointment, we would never grow or progress. My father always told us that "humans never learn," meaning that learning from others' mistakes is not something we do well. The trick is to learn from our own mistakes and mishaps and let the knowledge and wisdom we gain propel us to the next level of learning and understanding.

Let's take a look at what influence our circle provides and how it can impact us. First, fill your circle with people who are positive. The famous saying "misery loves company" should serve as a strong caution. Identify and be aware of negative individuals who come into your circle. Like a shark circling in the water, negativity can stealthily consume you if you're not alert. Bad attitudes will drain your energy, creativity, and drive and leave you empty. It's easy to join in negative conversations. We've all done it before, so be aware of the mood around you, and as soon as the conversation becomes negative, switch the direction and get the conversation back on track to something worthwhile, or simply walk away. After all, misery loves company, and it doesn't like a challenger.

Secondly, I have made it a point to never take advice from anyone who isn't experienced and successful in the area I'm trying to gain perspective on. This may sound harsh at first, but it makes sense if you think about it. For example, I wouldn't go to a gastroenterologist to get perspective on mental health. It's always better, in my opinion, to go straight to the source. I've seen too many friends experience bad outcomes because they acted on advice from well-meaning friends who were more clueless than they were about a situation. So if you want advice on starting a business, talk to people who have already walked the path you are on. I'm not saying that the individuals you get advice from need to have titles or diplomas, but they should have a deep wealth of experience, and more importantly, they should have achieved results in the area you are pursuing. I'm also not saying that I wouldn't listen to advice from other sources as well, but it does mean that I value it differently.

This advice-seeking practice started young with me. When I had a problem, my parents always provided their initial opinions and advice, but would then direct me to ask a person who had more knowledge on the subject than they did. This was an interesting parenting technique because they never claimed to be subject experts on any topic. Instead, they focused on whatever outcome we wanted to achieve and then encouraged us to seek those who had discovered the formula for success. There was no ego involved; rather, it was an unemotional, logical process. My parents wanted my brother and I to interact with people who had already "been there; done that." They also made it a particular point to send us to Cuban immigrants who had achieved success in their respective careers. They wanted us to learn from people who looked like us and spoke like us, and who had similar backgrounds. It was an ingenious move on their part because it was definitely easy to relate to them and see what our life could be if we were willing to put in the work. We never paid attention to those who hadn't made it or chose to embrace a victimhood mentality. In fact, anyone who came to our house claiming to be a victim in the freest country in the world were quickly put in their place. My father had no patience with and didn't tolerate anyone who ran from personal responsibility.

My parents' influence caused me to seriously consider potential friends at every stage of my life. When in elementary school, if a particular kid was a troublemaker, my parents discouraged us from associating with them. My parents not only wanted us to avoid any negative influences, but they understood that we'd ultimately be judged by our negative associations. Guilt by association may not be a popular concept, but there is truth in it. With time, I learned to put people through a subconscious interview process before I committed to a friendship with them. I studied their character by watching how they interacted with others and how they handled their surroundings. I paid careful attention to who was in their circle of influence as well. Your friends' friends can definitely have an impact as they provide influence, both good and bad. I did my best to fully vet them, and the results were well worth it. My friends were great role models to me. They cared about school, spoke respectfully to others, were a positive influence on others, and added value to society in general. Their parents were heavily involved in their lives and shared the same core values as my parents. My friends and I always encouraged each other to be the best we could be.

In the rare instance when a friendship devolved or I chose to follow a different path from a friend, I gave myself permission to move on. This sounds tricky to the younger generation who are immersed in cancel culture, but I believe that only in extreme circumstances should a friendship be ended outright. The better approach is to pull back gradually. Participate in social gatherings less, don't be available as readily, and detach emotionally, but still choose to be kind. Leave space for people to change and grow, and behave in such a way that if you interact socially with a former close friend, you can do so honestly and sincerely.

******

There was a time in college when my close group of guy friends and I started using the F word too casually. We were saying it carelessly in front of adults, women, and even children if we were out in public and unaware of our surroundings. When one of the guys realized this, he brought us together in a huddle and said, "Hey guys, I've noticed we've created this bad habit of dropping the F-bomb excessively, and it's becoming normal for us. You," he said, pointing at one of us, "just said it next to a professor the other day, and you," he said, pointing to another guy, "said it in front of my mom yesterday. Let's agree to take it out of our vocabulary so we don't have to think about where to use it." We felt the truth of what he was saying right away, and it was embarrassing. We knew we needed to be better. Our parents expected more of us, and we were finally mature enough to expect more of ourselves as well. We all agreed, and that was it. The F-bombs disappeared—forever.

I remembered that experience as I reflected recently on what a great group of friends I've had and the profound impact they've had on my life. We were young and free and under no parental supervision or obligation to say or do anything, and yet the moral compass ingrained in me (and my friends) couldn't be ignored. It was a crucial time in our development as we evolved from teenagers to men, and we chose to step up, not down, and the influence we had on each other was undeniable. We often think of peer pressure in a negative light, and it can be, but in my experience, the pressure I felt from my peers pushed me to grow and develop integrity. If someone in the group said "yes sir" or "yes ma'am" when addressing adults, we'd all do it. And here's the best part: the more proper and well-mannered we were, the more proper and well-mannered we knew we needed to be. It didn't go unnoticed either. People saw it and treated us differently. We were always happily received and genuinely complimented on our behavior, and it was inspiring to see the faces of my friends' parents light up with pride when we were around. My circle of friends made me a better person, and just when I thought I was doing great, someone inspired me to be even better. It was contagious in the best way possible. It felt good, and we were proud. We were walking in the light and helping each other progress along the way.

The only downside to developing a strong, tight-knit circle of friends is that if you choose to surround yourself with people who consistently make bad choices instead of good, you run the risk of being dragged down instead of being lifted up. For example, if everyone around you smokes marijuana excessively, is unmotivated, and has no plans for the future, that eventually becomes your normal. The same principle applies to study habits, church attendance, hygiene, ambition, communication, life planning, relationships, alcohol consumption, and even sexual habits. All aspects of life can either be positive and fulfilling or negative and draining. If you lose your ability to differentiate between behavior that is good or bad, you run the risk of losing control of the important decisions in your life, just as a drug addict loses the ability to make good choices. They become slaves to their addiction. However, when a person makes consistently good choices, their future becomes filled with unlimited potential. So tell me who you spend time with, and I'll tell you who you are.

CHAPTER 10

Partners and Parenting

*"We must raise up the next generation not for
ourselves but for society."*

I am often asked how my wife and I manage to have such a
nice and well-put-together family. How is it possible to have two
well-mannered, mild-tempered boys who people actually enjoy
being around? The truth is there's no instruction manual for
raising children, and I'm certainly not an expert. My brother and
I were raised in a loving and nurturing home, and my parents
have had a successful marriage for more than fifty years. My
upbringing laid the foundation for my future life, and I always
knew that I wanted my children to experience childhood in a
manner consistent with my own upbringing, and so far, that has
been the case. Even though I don't have all the answers to raising
a family, I have some ideas that might be useful. I've been told

that no experience is wasted, so the following is my advice to anyone looking for a partner they can create a home and start a family with.

Our lives are built on experiences, both good and bad. If a child is lucky enough to grow up in a loving and stable family, it's not hard to emulate the positive experiences they had. If, however, a child was raised in a dysfunctional or abusive environment, it's probably important to them as an adult to provide their children with an environment that's completely different from the one they experienced. It's no secret that children learn through observation, so they might live in a stable environment but witness a neighbor who is trapped in a domestic violence situation and be terribly affected by it. They might be friends with a child who is abused and experience part of the hurt and pain empathetically with them. On the other hand, a child's family might be terribly destructive, but they have a friend with a kind and loving family that welcomes them into their home and shows them how life could be different. Every experience in a child's life affects their development and shapes the way they perceive the world.

As a creative and curious child, I frequently paid attention to the environments and people in my life and analyzed them carefully. I liked to identify what qualities I shared with every family I interacted with. I made a subconscious list of which qualities were good and felt right to me and which ones didn't. Over time, certain characteristics became more prominent in my mind, and combining them with a determination to never settle for less than what I thought was ideal helped me develop a road map for my life. Once core ideals are established, it's time to find a person who shares the same values and morals as yours. After all, the more core values you share with your partner, the more intimate, strong, and harmonious your relationship will be. The problem with finding a partner is that people often don't know where to start looking.

Far too often, people trivialize the dating process and settle for far less than they'd hoped for in a partner. It's not uncommon to hear people rationalize, "This person is fine for now because we're not serious; we're just having fun." Even worse is when a person knows there are serious problems with a relationship but they decide to stay because "It's better than being alone." These justifications are dangerous because it's easy to get trapped in a bad situation. I like to compare this mindset to taking a puppy home. Everyone knows that once you bond with a puppy, it's extremely difficult to admit that the puppy isn't right for you, and it's even harder to return the puppy. You might have experienced this situation metaphorically in your own life, so you know how much more complex human relationships are in comparison to what I've just described. The bottom line is if you don't want a puppy (metaphorically), then don't bring one home! Once you clearly define what it is you're looking for in a potential partner, you need to go to places where that person can be found. For example, it's not reasonable to say that you'd like to marry a doctor and then hang out at the school of education looking for a possible partner. It just doesn't make sense.

Furthermore, everyone I know who's entered a relationship from places incompatible with their core values and beliefs, based on physical or sexual attraction alone, have all ended in disappointment, unhappiness, and heartbreak. Too many people waste years following this unproductive path, which is unfortunate considering it can easily be avoided. I believe that if you have a potential partner clearly defined in your mind and you do all you can to prepare yourself to be an equal partner, then when the right individual comes into your life, sparks fly. The law of attraction is a real thing, and it applies to just about every relationship in your life. Just make sure you're looking in the right place for the right person and, more critically, that you don't tie yourself to the wrong individual and then miss the opportunity to meet the person you were meant to be with.

As for me, I was always honest with myself about what qualities I was looking for in a wife. I wanted a Christian woman who had strong moral values and was interested in a traditional marriage. I have also always been politically conservative, so it was important to me that my future wife hold similar political views as well. Defining what's important in a potential partner is important because when a partnership is formed based on similar beliefs and values, the more likely it is that a successful, long-term marriage will be achieved. That's where true happiness is found. The choice is really very simple. What kind of ride do we want in life? A smooth one or a bumpy, painful mess?

Once common values are established, it's time to consider what the day-to-day interactions will be in a relationship. How will you treat each other? I spend a lot of time traveling, and sadly, I hear how many people speak to their partners with disrespect and contempt on the phone while walking through airports. I would be extremely unhappy if that language and tone were commonplace in my life. Jennifer and I have never verbally insulted each other, used profanity, or yelled at each other in a degrading or derogatory manner. Of course, we're not perfect people, and we do argue occasionally, but we don't "fight" with each other. When emotions run high, we walk away from the situation for a few hours until we're ready to regroup and apologize to each other. Apologizing is important because it acknowledges a willingness to forgive and move forward regardless of who's at fault. Interestingly, each time we apologize, we end up closer after the argument than we were prior to it. I think that's because every time we resolve a conflict, it proves that we can find a solution to any problem or uncomfortable situation if we're willing to work together to find it. I heavily credit Jennifer with the peace found in our relationship. Because I know how sensitive and nonconfrontational she is, I'm more aware of how to communicate with her because I never want my words or actions to cause her any undue pain. And although I may not get it right every time, she knows it's never my intent to hurt or insult her. Our marriage works because we always go back to the fact that we want a relationship based on love, compassion, and mutual understanding, which brings us happiness— attributes many couples don't experience or value enough to build a marriage on.

Once you have found an ideal mate and are well established in your relationship, you might start thinking about having children. Starting a family is a major commitment and shouldn't be taken lightly. Once a child arrives, there are no returns, and quitting is not an option. Being a parent is a lifelong commitment, one by which you commit to loving someone else more than yourself. Before you begin planning a family, however, you and your spouse should be in complete agreement on a number of very important points. How do you plan to raise your children? What cultural beliefs and traditions do you plan on embracing or letting go of? Do you plan to raise your children within the framework of a religion, and if so, are you in agreement on which one? How do you plan to financially provide for the needs of a growing family? How many children would you like to have? And on and on it goes. Being aligned with your partner is essential so there can be peace and harmony within the family unit. Because these questions are so important, couples should discuss them long before the relationship becomes serious. Leaving these important issues to chance or discovering a major disagreement late in a relationship is extremely risky.

It's also important to get the timing right before starting a family. Jennifer and I had enjoyed five years of marriage and had been together for a total of eleven years from the time we first started dating. We had entered a stage of our relationship where we were stable and well-adjusted to each other. We had moved beyond the phase of wanting to socialize constantly. There wasn't anything we needed to "get out of our system" that kids would hold us back from. We were ready to be "all-in" parents and give our children our full and undivided attention.

I always knew Jennifer would be an incredibly nurturing mother, and she in return was confident that that I would work hard and provide our family with the financial means necessary to live comfortable lives. On those issues, we were in complete harmony. We were also both big believers in structure and creating a physical environment our children would need to grow healthy—mentally, emotionally, and physically. We were particularly committed to healthy sleep schedules and calm and consistent daily routines. Some may read this and think our approach sounds excessive or rigid, but the truth was far from that. Everyone knows how difficult children can be when they're tired, hungry, or overstimulated, so we did all we could to provide an environment that minimized those situations. We honored naptime, kept to a consistent bedtime routine, and made sure meals happened at regular times throughout the day to keep tantrums to a minimum, if any at all. Most importantly, we committed to maintaining the routine seven days a week. We understood that if routines were disrupted, there would be unpleasant consequences, so we gave our kids the stability they needed to thrive. When we traveled, we did all we could to arrange our activities around our routines, which made the change of environment much easier on the kids. We also made it a point to go to church on Sundays as part of our regular weekend routine. We wanted our boys to understand the importance of taking time to honor God and acknowledge His hand in all things. Because of our intentional efforts and good management, we experienced much less drama during the infant and toddler phases of our children's lives than those around us. Looking back, it was truly a wonderful time that we will cherish forever.

Manners are another important aspect of parenting. As our boys began speaking, we always required them to say "please" and "thank you." They were never allowed to order anything without saying "May I please have . . ." to a waiter or attendant, and when they received their order, they were expected to say "thank you." There were no exceptions to these rules because we didn't want the boys to take anyone for granted—including their grandparents. I remember my mom telling me over and over, "They don't have to thank me; I'm their grandmother." I consistently responded, "Not every kid has a grandmother like you, so they must learn to be grateful for everything you do for them, even if it's only something very simple." Again, in this respect, our efforts paid off, and it's a beautiful thing to see children who don't feel entitled to everything.

Not everything about learning manners needs to be serious, though. I distinctly remember an interaction I had with my oldest when he was only four years old. I sneezed, so he called out, "God bless you, Daddy!"

I responded, "Thank you, Noah."

He then replied, "Thank you, Daddy, for thanking me."

We kept the thanking up for a while until we all laughed, but I smile when I remember that moment, knowing that true gratitude starts as a learned behavior, and so far our children have learned it well.

Other values we implemented in our home revolved around acceptable tones and attitudes. Jennifer is the most anti-drama-mama I have ever met, and God knows I don't like drama either, so our boys have followed us along those lines (either by example, DNA, or both). We've learned that it's important to keep a calm and detached approach when dealing with difficult situations. Problems generally arise when emotions run too high or we react too quickly to a situation. I think it's important for parents to model good behavior and lead by example. You can't expect your children to be calm and insightful if all they see are parents flying off the handle when things happen.

And finally, a spiritual upbringing has always been an important attribute in our home. Jennifer and I knew we didn't want our kids in public school as we felt there was more to a child's education than just academic studies. Although we live in an affluent community with excellent public and charter schools, we were adamant that our boys be taught daily in an environment that actively embraced Christian values, recognized the importance of spiritual development, and incorporated those values into the curriculum. This was important to us because we wanted our children to know and understand that we are all sinners and will always be, but God's love is real, and the pain of the world is only temporary. We wanted them to know that living a good, wholesome life is important and valuable, and if they lived life well, they could experience many blessings, as we have as a family. We wanted them to live a life of gratitude and feel a love that transcended their parents', going back to their Creator, who designed every aspect of them and the world we live in. I'm not here to push religion on anyone; however, I strongly feel that if you don't believe in something greater than yourself, and if you ignore the beacon within that consistently indicates that something bigger than us all must exist, you will begin to replace the notion of a Higher Being with money, power, or your own self-importance. If we're not careful, all these things can lead us to oblivion. The reality is that God exists whether someone believes in Him or not, and we need His presence in our lives. Exercising faith in Him unlocks lasting hope and peace in what would otherwise be a tumultuous life. And if, for the sake of argument, we find that nothing exists outside of life when all is said and done, at least we can feel good knowing that we spent our time here on earth being kind and loving, emulating the love of God and caring for others more than ourselves.

The biggest benefit we receive when we pick the right partner and we parent with intention is the lifelong support we receive from each other. Life is difficult, and it seems that it's meant to be that way. We grow through trials and difficulties, so we need to do all we can to make sure we have the support and resources we need, both physically and mentally, to survive whatever life throws our way. Everyone struggles with something. We all experience illness, sadness, death, and disappointments. Many of the things we experience are out of our control, so why not do all we can to make the things we can control as easy and as pleasant as possible? We can choose to be kind, loving, and compassionate (no matter what else is happening around us), but we also need to work at creating an environment where healthy emotions can prevail. Under these positive conditions, gratitude flourishes and our faith increases, which brings with it an abundance of peace and happiness.

Parenting is difficult, and I freely acknowledge that Jennifer and I don't always know if the things we're doing as parents are making a difference, but every now and then, we get a report card. It may come in the form of a cafeteria lady saying, "Your children are the most kind and cordial kids in the school," or a butler in Dubai commenting, "I just ran into your child by the pool, and the way he addressed me with kindness and gratitude was refreshing; we don't get that here often." It's those small moments that keep us on track and remind us that our efforts are not in vain and that we must continue to do all we can to teach our children in a well-rounded, thoughtful manner. After all, our children are our true and lasting legacy.

I once overheard my dad tell a friend that he and my mom didn't raise my brother and I for themselves; rather, they raised us for society. I was only thirteen years old when I heard that, and although I didn't fully comprehend what he was saying at the time, it opened my eyes to the fact that there was a higher purpose to what my parents were trying to teach us. With time and maturity, I began to see my father's words from society's perspective. We have a duty to ourselves and to others to live a higher standard. A society is only as good and healthy as its citizens, so we should aspire to be kind, decent, loving, and respectful, and most importantly raise up the next generation not for ourselves but for society.

CHAPTER 11

Privilege

"The only privilege we truly need to succeed is the privilege of being an American."

The word *privilege* was often used by my family when I was young. For my family, privilege was an inclusive concept; it could be achieved by anyone willing to work for it. My family is full of examples of what can be achieved through hard work and determination. Everyone in my family came to the United States with nothing and struggled through countless obstacles to advance. In the beginning, many of our parents didn't speak English well and were ridiculed for their heavy accents. The ones who came first had it the toughest as they had to forge a path for success without much guidance. Those who arrived later were fortunate to have examples to follow and just needed to emulate the example set before them. Our immigrant parents expected their children to go to college because they understood that education was the best way for us to advance and be successful. All around us were examples of Cubans who were living successful lives. They would tell you confidently that they had achieved the American Dream and enjoyed a personal level of success and a higher socioeconomic status. And the kicker is they did it as minorities, something we are told is not possible in today's society. We believe privilege is based on principles of hard work and integrity, which are nondiscriminatory by nature. Privilege is not reserved for the ruling class or a dominant race or ethnicity. Privilege is a pliable concept; it grows and expands over time, both within the immediate family as well as through future generations. In short, a person can achieve and expand a privileged status regardless of race or ethnicity, but only if they are willing to sacrifice, take risks, work hard, have a viable plan, and never give up.

Successful parents have taught children for generations that hard work rewards people of all races at any age in life. It is an important ingredient to the American Dream and has been proven to be true over many generations. Any parent, adult, politician, or educator who tells a child they are destined to fail or succeed based on their unique, immutable characteristics, despite their natural abilities and willingness to work hard, should be called out for child abuse. And yet, sadly, this is exactly what is happening. The hard truth is that success is not achieved without a tremendous amount of hard work and personal sacrifice. The evidence of this truth is all around us; just ask any successful person what they did to achieve their success, and the proof will be found in their answer. Anyone who uses race, gender, or age as an excuse for failure are being disingenuous and unfair to themselves and society in general. I understand that it can be extremely difficult to be honest and acknowledge personal failings and shortcomings. The natural human tendency is to make excuses and push responsibility onto anyone but ourselves. It's human nature, and human nature can be self-destructive. And the very worst part of it all is that misery loves company.

In the last several years, particularly after the Obama administration, the concept of privilege started becoming a mainstream buzzword in the political sphere. I found the timing of it curious. Over the last several years, the word privilege evolved into white privilege as our nation has become preoccupied with race as the primary reason for any outcome (whether the outcome is good or bad). Proponents of this concept are convinced America is a racist nation, and not being a racist is no longer good enough. You must be anti-racist—whatever that means. Of course, their reasoning is flawed. If we are indeed a fundamentally racist nation, then why did we elect a black man to the highest office in our land? It's ridiculous and laughable, and it's hard to take anyone seriously who thinks our nation and therefore its citizens are inherently racist. How could that have been accomplished if the United States as a whole is racist? How could we label all whites in the country racist when, according to the Pew Research Center, "more than three-quarters (76.3%) of all voters in 2008 were white" ("Dissecting the 2008 Electorate:

Most Diverse in U.S. History," April 30, 2009). If the white population in the United States is indeed full of racists, Barack Obama could not have decisively won the presidency in 2008. It simply would not have been possible. And eight years later, the first black vice president, Kamala Harris, was voted into office in an election with the most votes ever cast in our nation's history.

Although I am conservative and was disappointed that my political party didn't win in 2008, I remember the bittersweet feeling I experienced that election year. I vividly remember a sense of relief and pride on election night. Minorities in the United States and around the world could look to Barack Obama and say, "If he did it, anyone can too . . . and we now know America isn't racist!" It was an exciting time filled with hope and optimism. To me, the case for American racism was closed. America had finally achieved the dream Dr. Martin Luther King had so eloquently elucidated in 1963. The American people had spoken through the ballot box, and the message was loud and clear. We as a nation do not judge people based on the color of their skin, but rather we value eloquence, intelligence, and hard work, and are enamored by success stories wherein individuals overcome personal challenges. We value anything and everything that is good over race or ethnicity. The reality that Barack Obama could start from humble beginnings and achieve such stunning success at such a young age was inspiring, and when he won, we applauded. We celebrated and shared in the collective dream— the American Dream. I remember choking up on election night as I watched the news coverage, thinking America was forever changed for the better. What better reparations could the American people give to the black community than to elect a black man as president and then say, "Lead us!" It was a moment of light, truth, and hope that, unfortunately, took a violent turn into the dark and hateful period we find ourselves in now.

There are some people who, no matter how information is presented to them, refuse to let go of false beliefs. There are examples of this all around us. For example, the Flat Earth Society has increased their membership and following in recent years despite the mountain of indisputable scientific evidence collected over centuries that proves their theory to be incorrect. It's incomprehensible but a sobering reminder that for some, truth and reason do not matter. They function on raw feeling and emotion rather than logic and reason. Those who persist in referring to America as systemically racist, who believe it wholeheartedly, fall into this category. The evidence that proves that America is the least racist country in the world is staggering, but for some people, evidence is immaterial. And let me be totally clear, because I already know some are going to push back on my previous statement and say, "But look at so and so over there. . . . Aren't they racist?" Yes. Racism exists. Are there people who don't like Hispanics or other ethnic groups? Absolutely! I have encountered them, but they do not represent America as a whole. They are flawed individuals who have their own set of problems that have nothing to do with me or you. They certainly aren't stopping me from succeeding. If anything, it's clear to me that they are envious of success—

anyone's success—and they project their own self-hatred onto anyone who highlights their failings. Hate is a vehicle to make themselves feel better. We must not allow ourselves to internalize every hurtful comment because by doing so, the racism, bigotry, and hatred projected on us festers, grows, and eventually robs us of our peace and self-confidence. If we don't actively fight against it, hatred becomes reality and, like a malignant cancer, invades every aspect of life. Hatred, bigotry, and racism are weapons no one will use against me. I simply won't allow it.

I would like to share a personal example of how complex the concept of privilege has become. I've had several well-meaning "white" friends try to persuade me that I am oppressed because of my ethnicity. They tell me that being Cuban and a Latino (or as the woke would say, LatinX, a term I wholeheartedly reject) is a struggle that they are convinced they understand better than I do. In their eagerness to educate me, they speak down to me, insult my intelligence, and minimize my life experiences and accomplishments. They don't understand how I can't see what is so clear to them, that I am an oppressed minority who needs their help to recognize my oppression. The very thought is offensive. I may be a minority in the United States, but I'm certainly not a victim. When I question their illogical and insensitive statements, they reason that my problem is that I'm "more white" and am therefore an exception. They conclude that I simply don't know what it's like to be oppressed and therefore can't understand the struggle! At first, I laughed at how ridiculous this notion is, but as I realized how many people genuinely hold this misguided belief, I became angry and upset. And to make matters worse, they are unable to see how this line of thinking is exceptionally insulting. As a minority, I am expected to choose between being a victim or an oppressor. There are no other options. It's no wonder young minority children feel forced into choosing a side, and sadly, the younger generation has chosen victimhood. It's the path of least resistance. And imagine how white children feel; they don't even have a choice. They are automatically classified as oppressors, no questions asked. They epitomize the concept of "guilt by association."

Because I have worked hard, found success, and have strong conservative values, I am disqualified as a victim, and if I'm not a victim, I must be an oppressor and can no longer speak with authority. My lived experiences are no longer valid or valued. This is the new bigotry in America today. It is blatant, pervasive, and gaining in popularity. When I discuss this with my family and Cuban friends, they reassure me that people have lost their minds. We remind each other how grateful we are for our opportunities and even more grateful for the results, which we credit to God, because although we did the work, He ensured the blessings. We have all struggled. My grandparents' and parents' struggles became the struggles of the entire family. As close family members, problems were shared at the dinner table. We shared the hurt together, and what affected someone during the day hurt all of us spiritually and emotionally that evening. We were all occasionally bullied or encountered some form of discrimination at different times of our lives;

however, despite our personal challenges, we would never judge an entire nation based on the deplorable actions of a few.

The reality is that privilege exists in all countries and societies throughout the world. If you study the ultra-successful in America, for example, you will find that they have many common traits, and they are not related to race or ethnicity. For every Bill Gates, Warren Buffett, Megyn Kelly, or other successful Caucasian, there is a Barack Obama; Oprah Winfrey; Dwayne Johnson; Ben Carson; Lili, Gloria, and Emilio Estefan; Marco Rubio; Pitbull; and countless others. So if race isn't a common denominator, what is? The one thing every person listed above shares is that they are American citizens who have benefited from living in a free society where they had the opportunity to develop their skills and talents and have the legal right to benefit from them. America is the greatest nation on earth, and that's not because Americans are smarter or more talented than the citizens of any other country. What makes America special is that its citizens are free, free to dream big and pursue their interests, and they're also free to be lazy and unproductive. Either way, Americans choose for themselves who and what they want to be, and that choice alone, in my view, is a privilege. I understand it's hard for Americans who have never lived under oppressive government regimes to fully understand this. There may be a person living in Communist Cuba, Venezuela, or North Korea right now that has within them the knowledge and ability to cure cancer or solve the world's energy crisis, but they will never be able to do so because they are denied the opportunity to fully develop their talents because the totalitarian societies they live in do not value freedom and individuality.

Why should those who have taken risks, worked hard, and achieved great success be guilted and shamed for their success? A major component of the American Dream is to work hard and sacrifice so our children will have more opportunity and enjoy greater success than those who came before them. We may not all go at the same pace or enjoy the same level of success, but if properly focused, every individual and family can move forward. And with every success and step forward, new opportunities and experiences arise. This means that every new experience or opportunity allows you to grow exponentially and gain privilege. What makes America so special is that a child can come to the United States, not able to speak a word of English, have no financial advantages whatsoever, and then can still become a doctor, engineer, businessman, actress, or professor and achieve high levels of social and financial success. What I have just described is so commonplace in the United States that it doesn't occur to us that rapid upward mobility rarely happens in other countries (even the developed ones). When we understand how unique and exceptional America is and how limitless the opportunities are here, it's easy to realize that the only privilege needed to succeed here is the privilege of being an American. Even with our problems, America is still the best place on earth to achieve your highest potential.

Don't let anyone tell you that privilege is something reserved for the chosen few. The moment you accept that, you limit yourself and start to believe that you're incapable and unworthy of success. Reject (or cancel) any group or ideology that tells you that privilege is linked to immutable traits. That school of thought is rooted in racism and bigotry, and is undeserving of your time and energy. Rather, we should expand our knowledge of privilege and what it truly means. Most people have the privilege to see with their eyes, hear with their ears, speak with their mouth, and move their body freely. We are free to think for ourselves, to form opinions, and share them with others. We have the privilege to educate ourselves, work hard, live where we want to live, and choose how to live our lives.

You've had the privilege of reading this book and hopefully seeing life from a different perspective. What you do with that privilege is now up to you. I hope you are not influenced by or follow the popular trend of giving others the right to define your struggle. I hope you never give others the power to tell you what and how to think. Be grateful every day for the privilege and blessing of being free. That gratitude will open doors for you and provide endless opportunities if you have the courage to take them. And always remember: if you love America, she will love you back.

CHAPTER 12

Product of Your Environment

*"For some, their environment is transitionary, for others,
a permanent state of being; the choice is yours."*

As someone who has navigated life both by circumstance and choice, I have had the ability to see firsthand the role environments play in shaping our lives. I lived in a Communist country, and although I fled very young, my parents discussed it often as I was growing up, and it had a profound impact on my life. When my parents and I arrived in the United States, we lived in low-income housing, including a mobile home in a trailer park. As my family's circumstances evolved, I experienced upward mobility as we progressed from a lower-class community to an upper-middle-class neighborhood, and eventually to the most expensive zip code in the United States. I have attended multiple public schools, ranging from a school in a low-income neighborhood to those in middle-class and affluent communities. I have interacted and grown with the children of both environments and have witnessed firsthand what the differences are. Interestingly, I evolved professionally in much the same way. I began by working low-wage, part-time jobs, and then later navigated up the pay scale to corporate environments, both domestically and internationally, drastically increasing my pay. My cumulative experiences have given me a comprehensive perspective on how environments and social circles impact people's behavior, lifestyles, and the ability to progress and succeed.

As my family navigated along our American experience, I noticed that in most cases, the neighborhood a person is born into is the environment they're most likely to remain in. Many families and individuals living in low-income apartments, for example, are complacent about where they are and generally don't exude a lot of effort to improve their situation. My family, on the other hand, felt like temporary visitors in low-income housing. Our time there was temporary, similar to pausing for a break at a rest stop while on a long road trip. Our time at each stop wasn't in vain, nor was it wasted. There is something to learn at every step of life's journey, and only once those lessons are learned can one progress to the next phase of their life.

It is very clear to me that environments play a critical role in defining our progress, especially considering that we live and interact within multiple environments during the course of our daily lives. These environments include cities, neighborhoods, homes, schools, churches, jobs, and social circles. We should never underestimate the power of environments. School environments, for example, play a key role in a child's life as they are where they spend the majority of their day, just as work environments do for adults. In many ways, environments play just as large a role in shaping a person as interpersonal relationships do. For example, if a neighborhood is struggling with violence and there is no trust among neighbors, that becomes the dominant perspective that is shared by the people living there. This overarching perspective can affect how you approach situations at school or work, especially if you always feel that someone is out to get you.

With that in mind, environments should be considered carefully when choosing a profession or where you work. Some things to consider are the quality of a job's physical location. Is it in a good neighborhood where you feel safe? Will you interact with good people who are proficient and interested in your professional growth and development? Choosing well can propel you to continued and consistent success. Choosing poorly can lead to uncertainty, high levels of stress, and strained personal and family relationships. I recognize that there may be times when you might have to take a job that is less than ideal, especially if you're starting from humble beginnings, but if you find yourself in this circumstance, always keep an eye out for opportunities to improve your situation. If you find yourself in that situation, remember that if you can't envision where you want to be, then where you begin will likely be your final destination.

I got my first job in high school working for a

telemarketing company. My parents were hesitant for me to work because they felt my primary focus at that time was to do well in school, and they worried that a job would get in the way of that. They ultimately allowed me to take the job because I managed to work out a schedule that didn't compete with my school obligations. I had a four-hour shift two nights a week that ended by 8:00 p.m. and an eight-hour shift on Saturdays. I liked the job. I liked having a desk and being in a corporate environment, and I was excited that my hourly wage was a few dollars higher than the minimum wage at the time. I also enjoyed the people I worked with. They spoke well, showed up on time, and took their work seriously. Over time, however, I began to notice that my coworkers spent a lot of time discussing how they could increase their wage to $8 or $8.50 an hour. They talked about how if they became a supervisor, they would earn $10.50 an hour. This was a constant topic of conversation in the break room, and I remember almost falling into the trap of chasing the extra dollar until one day I realized that an extra dollar would amount to only four extra dollars at the end of my Tuesday shift. I began to contemplate how I could earn $20 an hour or more instead of focusing on how to make $8. I began thinking of the business as a whole, and the more I thought about it and what would truly make a difference in my life, I came to the conclusion that the position I was really interested in was that of the CEO or the majority shareholder.

With my new perspective, I began to view the behavior of my coworkers at the telemarketing company like rats fighting over a scrap of food. The reality is that some people will fight for scraps for years while others will simply settle for what they have and never aspire to more. Over time, the financial conversations in the break room became negative and transitioned to complaining about how they needed and deserved the extra dollar because they were drowning in debt. Listening to conversations like that long enough normalizes behaviors that would otherwise be unacceptable. You begin to think that everyone is underpaid and undervalued, that extreme debt is normal, and that only a "privileged few" can ever find true success. This toxic narrative diverts the blame from individuals and places it firmly on an unknown, unnamed, imaginary villain, and then that anger and frustration are spewed out on those in positions of power. Think about this scenario and compare it to every environment you've been exposed to throughout your life. What conversations did you have? What messages were broadcast to you? Were they positive or negative? Did they celebrate how amazing life is, or did they focus on how bad everyone has it? Whatever it was, your environment (good or bad) defined you and molded your thought process. The sad truth is that it's much harder to succeed when there's no clear path for you to follow.

When I graduated from high school, I had the unique opportunity to attend both a public community college and the University of Miami at the same time. My experience within the community college environment was particularly eye opening. Community college attracts people from all walks of life and socioeconomic backgrounds, although it was my observation that the majority of the students I attended class with were mainly low-income minorities. I remember that on the first day of every semester, classes were full, and everyone, for the most part, showed up. Within the first few weeks, however, class sizes started to dwindle as assignments were given and test dates put on the calendar. I began to hear students say, "I'm too busy working; I don't think I can do this"; "I don't like this professor"; or "I'm not sure I can pass this class." And then, right before the cutoff period when you could drop a class without paying a fee, students began dropping like flies. Sadly this ritual was repeated every term and became a normal part of my community college experience. In contrast, my University of Miami experience was a completely different story. It was very rare for a student to drop a class, and dropping out of the university altogether was extremely rare. In fact, I observed that when classes became challenging, UM students paused their social life to make sure they had enough time to complete and excel on their assignments. During final exams, most students stopped going out with friends and limited their non-school-related activities so they could do well. It was interesting to me to see the contrast and dynamics between these two worlds.

Even with the environmental differences highlighted right in front of me, I'll admit that I fell into some lazy habits while I attended community college. I never considered quitting school, but I did drop a class from time to time. The problem is that if a student drops four classes in a two-year period, they fall one semester behind, and most students who drop classes end up keeping only one or two classes a semester. That's why it generally takes students so long to get through community college. Luckily for me, I quickly realized I was becoming a product of my environment and committed to changing my mindset to one where my new normal would be an "all-in" approach that would guarantee a timely graduation and subsequent transition to an environment where everyone shared the same positive approach to school. With my newfound attitude and perspective, I allowed myself zero excuses or further delay. I reasoned that for every year I delayed getting a degree, it would cost me hundreds of thousands of dollars in future income. People who never learn to take control of their lives and choose the best environments have a difficult time recovering when life's challenges arise.

Remember that if you immerse yourself in positive environments to work and live in, you will have more control of your life and have a better chance of achieving positive outcomes overall. More importantly, you should do all you can to create positive environments. At home and in your social circles, surround yourself with good people who bring out the best in you, and be a good friend in return. Be on time. Listen to others, be a good mentor, and find ways to progress. In your work environment, you should always be looking for ways to excel and enhance your career by proving your value to those who have the authority to advance you. This forward-thinking mindset puts you on track to keep progressing while gaining the knowledge you'll need to achieve the next level of success. As you continue traveling along your professional or technical track, you'll understand that you have the power and ability to forge the path that's right for you. You are in control, and the moment will suddenly come when you realize that you are the captain of your own ship, not a passenger on someone else's or, worse, on a raft drifting aimlessly with no means to steer yourself.

Never forget that you are free to live your life as you wish, and it is your right to do so. That's the gift and beauty that America offers: that dreams can come true, although success usually occurs incrementally. While you're chasing your dreams, never forget that freedom comes with responsibility—and you must be the sole author of your choices. In my experience, successful people take their responsibilities seriously, they know the outcomes they would like to achieve, and they choose their environments carefully in order to ensure they can achieve those outcomes.

CHAPTER 13

Self-Confidence – *No Time for Victimhood!*

"Self-confidence is the only remedy to insecurity, doubt, and perceived oppression."

I t seems that recently our nation has gone from celebrating the success of others to blaming others for the fact that not everyone experiences equal amounts of success or any success at all. As an immigrant whose family came here with literally nothing other than a desire to be free, I find this attitude to be appalling and pathetic. From my perspective, native-born citizens (from all walks of life) have a tremendous advantage compared to those who arrive here with nothing other than the clothes on their backs. To see so many American citizens genuinely believe that they are victims of oppression is in my opinion a clear defilement of the American promise.

Dennis Prager, a prominent writer, social commentator,

and radio talk show host, frequently says that to understand America, you must first understand American values. The three American values Prager identifies are *e pluribus unum, liberty,* and *in God we trust.* The first, *e pluribus unum,* is a Latin term that means "out of many, one." This is the American motto that was created shortly after our nation's founding in 1776 when the thirteen original colonies joined together to form a new nation. Over time, as the country grew in size and population, e pluribus unum began to represent one people with various backgrounds and beliefs, and it's a concept that continues to hold true today. American immigrants assimilate faster and more fully than immigrants in other countries. This is partly due to the excitement of finally making it to America but is also due to the fact that the American people are generally very welcoming and accepting of immigrants. In fact, the moment an immigrant is sworn in as a citizen of the United States, they are instantly considered American in every way and enjoy equal status to every other citizen in the land. This is a mindset unique to the United States. In most European countries, a person's ethnic background defines their status and involvement in society far more than their citizenship, which has been a significant factor for ethnic tensions throughout the world.

The next value, *liberty,* is an often undervalued and misinterpreted concept. Liberty can be defined as being free from oppressive restrictions imposed by authority on one's way of life, behavior, or political views. We all agree that certain rules or laws must be followed in order for society to function well, but generally speaking, in America, people are free to speak their thoughts and live their lives the way they deem fit. We are not the only country to value liberty, but we understand liberty differently from other countries. For example, many countries restrict personal liberty in an attempt to achieve equality. In America, we believe that all human beings are born equal and therefore are entitled to equal treatment under the law. America is built on the assumption that every citizen enjoys equal opportunity but not necessarily equality of outcome. Of course, America has not always lived up to this value. We have historically failed in many ways, but as we've tried to fix our problems and learn from our mistakes, America has become the freest and most tolerant country on earth today. We believe that a person can go as far as their ability, work ethic, or even luck takes them. Everyone can choose the path that's right for them. If the government limits personal liberty in an effort to achieve equal outcomes —by regulating income, for example—that would be the end of liberty. In a free society, doctors earn a high salary for their knowledge and skills, athletes are paid millions for their physical abilities, and teachers will make far less but enjoy the perk of working nine months out of the year. Having liberty means being able to choose your own path and own the consequences of that choice, and any attempt by the government, or any other entity, to control outcomes diminishes liberty for all.

The last value that Prager mentions, and in my opinion the most important, is in God *we trust*. While America does not have a sanctioned state religion, there's no denying that our country is founded on and is heavily rooted in Judeo-Christian principles and values. The Declaration of Independence clearly states that "all men . . . are endowed by their Creator with certain unalienable Rights, that among these are Life, Liberty and the pursuit of Happiness." That statement is a clear acknowledgement that rights come from God, not from men. The recognition that rights come from God is important because if our rights come from men, then men could also take them away. Accepting and acknowledging this basic tenet of the Constitution prevents any individual, organization, or government from placing their desires, values, and beliefs above our own.

American values are the reason that the United States has become the freest and most prosperous country in the world. With such a strong success record, I find it completely alarming that many Americans want to fundamentally transform our current system. Part of that transformation is a push to celebrate and identify individuals based on ethnic, racial, or even sexual preferences, which is in direct opposition to the concept of "out of many, one." They want to force equality without acknowledging that segregating people into identity groups reduces individual freedom instead of advancing it. And most concerning of all, they want to remove God as the source of morality and rights. While I respect an individual's right to their personal beliefs, I can't fathom why anyone would turn against the values that formed the foundation of such a wonderful country that allows people to live their lives according to their beliefs and individual values.

Identity groups aren't necessarily bad, though, especially if they're established on common actions as opposed to immutable physical or ethnic characteristics. After all, we can all agree that as a society we don't value drug dealers, criminals, or bullies. We do, however, admire first responders, humanitarians, and caregivers. Once we have broad agreement on that, we can begin to judge people on their individual merits and not their group identity. As Americans, we are losing our way by splitting ourselves into different groups, and anything that pulls us apart prevents us from identifying as one. I think people of every race, ethnicity, and background have accomplished and achieved incredible things. Yes, America has historically been predominantly white and will therefore showcase a lot of Caucasian accomplishments, but to focus only on Caucasian achievements does a disservice to Hispanic, Asian, and black Americans who have attained prominence and success as well. You don't have to look too hard to see it. The evidence of minority success is all around us. And if you look even closer, you will find common traits that all successful people share that have nothing to do with ethnicity, race, or any other factor. Success starts and ends with a mindset.

Another alarming trend that has developed recently is self-censorship. Freedom of speech works only if people feel that they can communicate their thoughts and feelings without recrimination. However, in the era of cancel culture, people are self-censoring and refraining from talking about difficult issues and declining to describe people by their physical or ethnic features for fear of being accused of being a racist. We're teaching ourselves to be silent, and if this trend continues, we won't be able to recognize truth, and if we can't recognize and acknowledge truth, then we lose the ability to help others and effect meaningful change. For example, some would consider it racist to say, "The majority of children born out of wedlock are disproportionately represented by the black and Hispanic communities and are therefore more likely to experience generational poverty because of it." It doesn't matter that the facts support the statement; our fear of being judged or accused of racism keeps us quiet, deflecting light from this important issue. Instead, we should be discussing difficult issues like this one and work towards solutions to meaningfully help the people we are too scared to offend.

Coming from a Communist country, I find It hard to imagine why anyone would want to dismiss American values. When my family came to the United States, they readily adapted to the American way of life, so much so that they were surprised that there were people who wanted to diminish or discard it. It shows a lack of understanding and a tremendous amount of ignorance and naïveté about the consequences of abandoning American values. It's painful to see the nation being divided and resegregated into racial, ethnic, and other identity groups. The obsessive need to label people as oppressors or oppressed is truly disheartening, and even more alarming, these ideologies seem to be enthusiastically taking root within American society. It's baffling to me because the general attitude among Cuban immigrants is that anyone can overcome nearly any obstacle *if* they're willing to work hard and make the necessary sacrifices to get to where they want to be. Most Cuban Americans don't tolerate a victimhood mentality, and those who claim it are not given a platform because as a community, we understand that the only Cuban victims are those living under the tyrannical Communist government in Cuba.

The reality is that we live in a society largely free from oppression, systematic or otherwise. The oppression people feel today is mainly self-imposed and fueled by fear from those who profit from this narrative. The truth is that if anyone feels oppressed, they have no one to blame but themselves because oppression, in my opinion, is a state of mind. This country allows the same general opportunities to all who live here. Of course, some start off with more than others, but having an affluent background isn't necessarily a guarantee of success, just as being poor doesn't necessarily condemn an individual to a life of poverty. If you look at a high school in a diverse community like the one I attended, you'll find high achievers and low achievers, but you can't accurately predict who they'll be based on race or affluence alone, and blaming one group for the failings of another is ludicrous.

I have personally encountered people who didn't like me based solely on the fact that I'm Hispanic. It would be easy to accuse all Caucasians of discrimination, but the reality is that many of the people who have discriminated against me were of other minority groups. I have come to accept that there will be people who don't like me, for whatever reason, and that's okay. We don't have to like everyone we come in contact with, and we can't expect to be liked by everyone. That's simply not reality, and it's not fair to stereotype entire groups of people based on our individual experiences with a select few. Painting with too broad a stoke is dangerous. For example, if all whites are oppressors, then are all Hispanics illegal immigrants who are intent on taking advantage of the American welfare systems? It goes both ways. If there is a white supremacist who hates minorities, it would be unfair to pin white supremacy on the vast majority of Americans who are white. We cannot define any group, or America generally, by its least common denominator.

On a personal level, I don't have time for the victimhood narrative. I'm a busy person, and I choose to focus my time and energy on my career, loved ones, and humanity in general. I don't have the patience or desire to waste time interacting or arguing with people who don't like me or who want me to believe that I'm oppressed. If you allow those kinds of narratives to dominate your life, it will stifle your growth and distract you from the things that really matter. Don't surrender your power to any person or ideology that offers nothing meaningful in return. If you look at those who have gone down that road, it's easy to see the effect. They are miserable, angry people who constantly blame others for their failings and shortcomings. They claim to have deep insight and understanding as to how the world really works, but they lack empathy and compassion towards those who disagree with them. I'm not denying that there's real injustice in the world today, but how we handle those situations shows us who we really are and, more importantly, what we're made of.

Victimhood, in my opinion, is a choice. I'm not referring to serious legal situations here such as rape, abuse, or assault. Those crimes should never be tolerated in a civil society. What I'm referring to is the belief that a person can never succeed because of some immutable characteristic that they possess. I believe that you become the product of your thoughts. The victimhood mentality is heavily invested in creating groups of oppressors and oppressed, so if you go through life believing that you're a victim, that's exactly what you'll become. If you believe you'll never get ahead because you're Hispanic, then you won't, and if you buy into that mentality, you not only become oppressed but become your own oppressor.

My family has experienced injustices just like everyone else. We have been denied service because of our accents, pulled over for minor infractions, and many other frustrating, and clearly unfair, situations. Not everyone we come into contact with will act in good faith, but we never use those experiences to define and judge an entire group. Uncomfortable interactions are simply that . . . uncomfortable. The best approach is to acknowledge the injustice, report it (if necessary), and move on. Our mentality is that ignorant and rude people are annoying, but at least they're not Communists. Unlike Communists, the only control they have in our lives is the control we give them.

Self-confidence is the only remedy to insecurity, doubt, and oppression. If you take responsibility for yourself and believe you can achieve whatever goal you set your heart and mind to, anything is possible as long as you're willing to do the work.

You've got to walk the walk, and if someone gets in your way, walk around them. Never allow a setback or challenge be the reason to abandon the work you're doing to improve your life or, even worse, forsake the progress you've already made. Positive choices must be made daily if you don't want to slide back into destructive habits that won't get you where you want to be. When you truly value yourself and acknowledge your worth, your confidence grows and you gain the mindset you need to vanquish the oppressor, both within and without. Only then will excuses end and the victim mentality cease to exist, leaving space for growth and wisdom to flourish.

CHAPTER 14

NO! to Socialism

"People don't learn from other people's mistakes."

I grew up during the era of Ronald Reagan, and it seemed that based on Reagan's decisive election victories, conservative ideology was widely embraced by the country at that time. It was a refreshing change for my family to arrive to the United States from Cuba during the era of Reagan. It was a time when the principles of personal liberty and freedom were emphasized, which was exhilarating to my parents and extended family after living under a Communist regime. My family has now been in the United States for more than forty years, and so much has changed since then. The government has grown in size and power, and the thirst for more authority and control through all levels of government across the country seems to be growing.

My dad likes to say that "people don't learn from other people's mistakes." That statement is true on a personal and governmental level. In fact, you could say that "governments don't learn from other governments' mistakes." Just as with most failed governments, the more power and authority it is given, the larger it grows and the more it requires ever-increasing amounts of money to sustain itself. Any opposition it encounters must be stopped in order for it to continue to thrive. It's like a snowball that descends downhill slowly at first, but as it gains momentum, it becomes unstoppable, growing in speed and size, destroying anyone and anything that crosses its path until there's nothing left.

I remember a time when Bernie Sanders was a minor player in the political arena. He was generally considered a comical figure who was mocked but never given any serious consideration. He openly embraced socialism, vacationed in Communist Russia during the Cold War, and applauded Communist revolutions in Cuba and Venezuela. When he was elected mayor of Burlington, Vermont, in 1981 (by ten votes), his beliefs were considered fringe and unacceptable, and yet four decades later, he became the runner-up for the presidential nomination of the Democratic Party. How can a socialist, with values so antithetical to the values espoused by the American Constitution, rise to prominence and find safe haven and support for his radical political ideals in the United States?

A Gallup poll conducted in 2019 found that 43 percent of Americans think socialism would be a good thing for the country.

The percentage is even higher for women, minorities, and, most concerning, young people (Kay C. James, "Building a Movement to Stop 'Democratic Socialism,' Heritage Foundation, October 23, 2019). What has happened? What are we teaching our youth? How can they not see that government programs always come at a cost, even when they're promoted as "free?" Unfortunately, our youth have very little knowledge or personal experience with paying taxes, managing budgets, and running large-scale programs. They cannot grasp the simple truths of socialism. They don't understand the fundamental flaw with socialism that Margaret Thatcher succinctly explained: "Socialist governments traditionally do make a financial mess. They always run out of other people's money" (Interview, This Week, Thames TV, February 5, 1976). The reality is that socialism has failed in every country in which it has been tried. Unfortunately, young people today feel that socialism hasn't been implemented correctly, and in their arrogance and lack of experience, they believe that they and their generation can somehow do it better. It's a frustrating circular conversation that proves what my dad always said is right: people don't learn from other people's mistakes.

It is an accepted fact that socialism rejects the dignity of individuals, embraces the state, and spends all its time and energy in growing the power of government through control. Conservative principals, in contrast, are directly opposed to the principles of socialism. Conservatives believe in small government, limited power, and individual freedom. Our Founding Fathers understood the corrupting nature of power, so they put safeguards in place (they called them checks and balances) to limit power. Those societal safeguards, however, have been eroding for years, and when we can no longer agree on the basic principles that should govern society, our unalienable rights to life, liberty, and the pursuit of happiness make way to the "greater good" mentality of socialism.

We can loosely compare modern America society to the fictional construct of Pride Rock in *The Lion King*. The movie depicts two extremes. On the one hand are lions who work hard, provide for their families, and maintain law and order through honest leadership. Hyenas, on the other hand, are conspiratorial, lazy, and refuse to work or contribute meaningfully, but instead cause havoc and take what is not rightfully theirs. In the story, the hyenas overtake the lions and disrupt the social and natural ecosystems, causing ruin and destruction. The lions eventually revolt and overtake the hyenas, restoring order and peace throughout the land, but that healing and restoration took time and concentrated effort. Similarly in our modern world, anyone who is promised free food and money with no expectation to work or contribute to society puts the stability of our entire nation at risk. Again, reiterating Margaret Thatcher's previous quote, "The problem with socialism is that you eventually run out of other people's money." Socialism is unsustainable both morally and economically, especially when its programs promote and increase the number of individuals who rely on government, thereby creating more takers than producers.

It is my belief that Americans, for the most part, don't

pay close attention to national or international affairs. We are a country focused on current events and frivolous entertainment, and the way we consume news seems to prove the point. For the most part, people read headlines and ignore the deeper content, a fact well understood by social media and news outlets. A significant amount of time and effort are put into writing sensational headlines because the media wants to persuade and control your thoughts in only a few words. They do this knowing that readers won't take the time to become properly informed. This practice is deceptive, manipulative, and calculating. It is irresponsible and should not be tolerated. It's like being a member of a corporate board who doesn't bother to read the proposals the board is going to vote on. The title may say "Acquire Company X with 5,000 Employees" and the board replies, "Great! How nice! I vote yes to grow our empire," without realizing that the company they're voting on would put their entire enterprise out of business because it is unprofitable and unsustainable. This is what we do as voters, and this is what Congress does as well when they pass bills.

Congress votes on a bill's "headline" because it feels good and then are shocked to learn that the bill contains more poison than honey. House Speaker Nancy Pelosi summed this up nicely when the Patient Protection and Affordable Care Act (Obamacare) was brought up before Congress for a vote in March 2010. Consistent with headline culture, the name of the bill was purposely misleading regarding the substance and purpose of the bill, and regarding the content, she famously said, "You've heard about the controversies, the process about the bill…but I don't know if you've heard that it is legislation for the future – not just about health care for America, but about a healthier America, but we have to pass the bill so that you can find out what is in it – away from the fog of the controversy."

In my opinion, the manner in which the bill was brought forward was irresponsible. I strongly believe that when a large piece of legislation is presented that affects all Americans, it should not be allowed to pass without bipartisan support and more importantly, there should be an adequate amount of time allocated for the bill to be properly studied before it is voted on. At the time of its passing, the majority of Americans were not in favor of the Patient Care and Affordable Care Act, especially as details about the bill began to surface and concerned citizens began to panic. The Affordable Care Act, as it turned out, was actually unaffordable and didn't live up to the promises politicians made on its behalf. Contrary to what was being promised, citizens wouldn't be able to keep their doctor or their health plan; it didn't save families thousands of dollars, and in fact, the cost of healthcare increased. And perhaps the most concerning deception occurred when Americans were falsely informed that the Affordable Care Act would not be a tax, when in reality it was.

If you were to sit down with a fellow American with an openly different political viewpoint and take the time to break down an issue, you would likely find that the majority of self-identified liberals don't actually agree with what they're voting for. I have found this to be true with my own conversations, and to further add credence to this point, the Heritage Foundation asked a mix of conservative, moderate, and liberal young adults if they could find something to like about conservative ideology. Only 39 percent responded favorably. They then asked how they felt about smaller government and giving more power to individuals and communities versus creating more government programs. The same individuals who had generally negative views of conservatives increased in favorability and agreement from 39 percent to 63 percent regarding specific conservative principles and policies. The same question was posed to members of the Hispanic community, and the rates went from 38 percent to 61 percent. For African Americans, it went from 24 percent to 57 percent. This poll demonstrates that Americans broadly agree with conservative positions but get distracted and divided on issues due to headline talking points (Kay C. James, "Building a Movement to Stop 'Democratic Socialism,'" Heritage Foundation, October 23, 2019).

Proponents of socialism believe that the previous outcomes of socialist nations will never happen in America. Many believed that Venezuela would never fall to socialism, but of course, that's exactly what happened. I personally know people who voted for socialism in Venezuela who later escaped and came to America to avoid the consequences of their poor choices. I think it's important for people to understand that what happened in Venezuela will likely happen in America if we don't take charge of the political narrative and push for proper historical education. We need to teach our youth the principles of Karl Marx, the founding father of socialism, and explain how those principles have failed in every country where they've been tried. Socialism promises a society free from class, but the reality is that socialists give themselves elite status and assume the role of the ruling class. It's an ideology rooted in lies, ignorance and hypocrisy, and anyone who believes otherwise is either naïve, uninformed, or has aspirations of being part of the ruling class.

President Reagan famously said, "Freedom is never more than one generation away from extinction. We didn't pass it to our children in the bloodstream. It must be fought for, protected, and handed on for them to do the same, or one day we will spend our sunset years telling our children and our children's children what it was once like in the United States where men were free." Every year, we see our education system move further away from conservative principles. The prime example of this is how universities suppress free speech by censoring conservative voices on campus. And unfortunately, the indoctrination reaches down into middle school and, in some cases, elementary school as well. I specifically remember when my seventh-grade teacher spent an entire day lecturing the class about the benefits of Communism. As you might imagine, dinner didn't go well that night when I told my parents what I had learned. More recently, Marxist ideologies have been repurposed into new ideologies such as critical race theory, the 1619 Project, and other pro-socialism curriculums used to teach our youth to despise America. We got to this point because conservatives believe in free speech and allow people to express whatever they want. The Conservative approach is to simply disagree and then move on. Socialists, on the other hand, don't give the same courtesy to conservatives. They know they must shut down conversations entirely so that they can control the messaging and narrative of any situation in order to gain and maintain power over the hearts and minds of Americans.

We must fight back against socialist ideals wherever they are manifested. We need to teach our children that it is a privilege to live in America regardless of whatever social class they identify with. Even the poorest person in American has advantages that aren't available to people in other countries throughout the world. We need to teach the truth of American history—including both the good and the bad. As a country we have made mistakes, but we've also worked hard to acknowledge and fix them. The reality is that the promise of America, as detailed in the *Declaration of Independence*, is that all people are created equal and are entitled to life, liberty, and the pursuit of happiness. Our children need to understand that our rights come from God, not the government, and the primary role of government is to secure those God-given rights for its citizens so they have the freedom and discretion to live life as they please.

Socialist ideology must be fought head-on wherever it's found. My family suffered and sacrificed everything they had to get to America. I'm humbled that an entire generation of my family was willing to suffer so that subsequent generations— mine included—could enjoy a life of freedom, opportunity and prosperity. It would be tragic beyond belief if my family ended up where they started. America is truly the last bastion of freedom and liberty in the world, and if she is destroyed, we will have nowhere to go. Individual dignity and ideals won't matter and will become irrelevant without the ability to express ourselves freely. If socialism takes hold in our country, America's youth will never have the opportunity to realize their full potential, and the pursuit of happiness—the American Dream—will cease to exist. If that happens, our nation will inevitably be transformed into an American Nightmare, and we must not let that happen.

Acknowledgements

This book would not be possible without my family; beginning with my grandfather, **Gerardo Bello**, whom I greatly admired. His hard work, determination and resolve to live beneath his means allowed him to build financial security for his family and realize the America Dream on a factory salary. I would like to acknowledge and thank my parents, **Leyda** and **Gerardo Bello Jr.** whose words, wisdom, and careful nurturing made me the man I am today. There are no adequate words to express the love I have for them, nor the profound gratitude I feel for all they've done for me. They are my heroes, and everything I've achieved I freely attribute to them.

My professional success would not be possible without the steadfast love and unwavering support of my wife, **Jennifer Bello**, who has stood by my side since we were young college students and always encouraged me to pursue my dreams. Jennifer is a wonderful woman, a talented teacher and an exceptional mother to our children, **Noah** and **Evan**, who are my pride and joy. Fatherhood is the greatest gift Jennifer has ever given me, and being a father has deepened my understanding of unconditional love and has provided me deeper purpose and meaning in my life. Our family exists because of Jennifer, and I am forever grateful she took a chance on me.

I'd like to express my appreciation and gratitude to my extended family, friends and colleagues who have consistently supported and encouraged me along the way. Many have been an integral part of my story and provided words of wisdom and encouragement at pivotal moments throughout my life.

I would like my brother, **Sanders Bello**, to know how much I love and rely on him. Our shared upbringing means he understands me better than anyone else, and I cannot imagine my life without him by my side. I am truly fortunate to have him as my brother.

Barbara Wasaacz has the uncanny ability to sense when I need an encouraging phone call or text message. She always knows the right thing to say to bring a smile to my face. I couldn't imagine living in a world without her as my friend.

Ronnie Khalil is another long-time friend who has always kept it real with me and was instrumental in designing the cover of this book. I appreciate his honest friendship and wicked sense of humor. I hope we wind up in the same nursing home one day.

I have several business partners who I admire greatly, and who have been an integral part of my life. Business partnerships are just as meaningful and complicated as any other relationship, and I feel very fortunate to have partnered with talented people who share my work ethic, work well together and always make the best of any situation. We've had an exhilarating business run together and I wouldn't trade a single one if I had to go back and do it all over again.

There is, however, a specific business partner who merits special acknowledgment. **Michael McCauley** has been more than a business partner to me, he has been a true friend and a person I freely acknowledge as family. From the day we met, he trusted and welcomed me into his aviation life, which gave me opportunities I would never have had otherwise. May our journey together live on.

I want to thank my publishers **TJ Hoisington** and **Troy Dunn** who have become my friends. Their interest and commitment to my story and philosophy of life made this book possible. What started out as a dinner conversation turned into a book that will be a lasting legacy for me and my family.

A very special thank you to **Jenny Parkin**, who worked tirelessly as my right hand for more than a year to keep the project moving forward. This book would not have happened without her diligent involvement in challenging me to dig deeper and organize my thoughts properly.

And finally, I would like to acknowledge and thank several teachers who unknowingly altered the course of my life. **Mr. Leonardo Villar**, my middle school **Band Director**, was the first teacher to believe in me and give me a leadership role. His confidence in me set me on the path to success. **Mr. Steven**

Gardner, my high school Band Director, made me the first male Drum Major the school had had in decades. His timing was providential and came at a moment when I was struggling to know exactly where I belonged. His belief and approval of me brought me out of the tail end of the darkest time of my adolescent life. Lastly, **Mr. Michael Mann**, the band director at the University of Miami, allowed me to continue my real-world leadership training when he elected me to be Drum Major of the "Band of the Hour" Marching Band – a role that provided more practical value and experience than any college class I ever took.

When I felt like the world was against me, these three men strengthened me and gave me the chance to grow and develop beyond anything I thought possible. They truly embody what dedicated teachers can do for humanity and demonstrate the importance of preserving and promoting music and the arts in schools - because sometimes music and the arts are the only thing that gets some of us through.

Thank you all, from the bottom of my heart.

About Fabian Bello

Fabian Bello was born on September 2, 1976 in Havana, Cuba. At the age of 2, he, along with his parents and paternal grandmother left the island enroute to Madrid, Spain, where they waited several months before obtaining the Visas needed to immigrate legally into the United States of America. On September 27, 1979, only 25 days after his 3rd birthday, he, along with his family entered the US and started his and their journey towards the American Dream. On that day, he was indeed (Re)Born.

Without a dollar to their name, other than the clothes on their backs, they started fresh in a free country that would promise prosperity with hard work and good choices. They lived in rental apartments to start, and even a mobile home to save enough for a down payment for/on their first home. Within 5 years, they were homeowners and more importantly, American Citizens. Fabian attended lower-middle-class public schools in the cities of Homestead, Hialeah, and Hialeah Gardens. Upon graduation, he went to Miami Dade Community College for his Associates in Arts, then transferred to the University of Miami for his Bachelors in Business Administration.

He started his career as a Marketing Manager and quickly ascended through the professional ranks, becoming the youngest individual to ever have a Director position in a company of over 15,000 team members at the time, overseeing Operations, Business Processes and Quality. Within a decade he was already in the C-Suite, holding various positions as Executive Vice President, COO, to ultimately become President, CEO and Chairman of various aviation companies. As President and CEO, he has been responsible for over half a billion USD in revenue within the first decade in those leadership roles. Total personnel count exceeds 500 individuals with over 1,000 at one point in their careers under his leadership. Fabian feels great responsibility to ensure the well-being of each and every single team member and all those who make their business possible. He is always aware that the responsibility transcends the team member and impacts their respective families.

Fabian's story is remarkable, although he feels it is a similar story to most immigrants and doesn't think it is that special at all. However, what he finds extraordinary are the many Americans who have excuses of why they can't, couldn't or haven't, while having exponential privilege that an immigrant